CUTTING OFF:

Life As A Postman

Lance Manley

∞ CUTTING OFF ∞

∞ CUTTING OFF ∞

Copyright © 2017 Lance Manley.

All rights reserved.

ISBN-13: 978-1541106352

ISBN-10: 1541106350

∞ CUTTING OFF ∞

Also by the author...

1. Stab Proof Scarecrows
2. Cowboy
3. Alaskadie and the Seal of Rock & Roll
4. Warlord and Twinkle
5. Two Princes
6. Walk in Pieces: *Diary of a Krav Maga Practitioner*
7. Adolescent Incandescence

With Diana Aquino:

- The Cockroach Effect: *Life in the Tampico Drug Wars*
- El Efecto Cucaracha *(Spanish translation)*

As LR Manley (for older children and young adults):

The Tales of Alegria

Book I- The Catastrophe of the Emerald Queen
Book II- The Sunder of the Octagon

∞ CUTTING OFF ∞

∞ CUTTING OFF ∞

Acknowledgements

To colleagues who made this job bearable:
Paul Rose, Paul Hopgood, Craig Waters, Dave Watters,
Not-Dave, Chris White, Alison the Milfy Manager, Shane
Forward, Gary Cross, the Newey Twins, Jason King,
Shakey, Steve Lafferty, Cynthia DOM, Bali (sp?), Kevin
Massey, Christina Reece, Jay Hey, Neil Compton, Tom
Burke, Glenn Simmons, Simon Kirkland, Ripper, Jason
Shorts, Fraaan, Steven-Stephanie-Steven, and the long
suffering Archie.

To those in very senior management whose
tomtwattery led to this book being written.

To Danny Armiger for forgiving Indiana Jones.

To the receptionist at No.4

To Rupert the Westie

∞ CUTTING OFF ∞

∞ CUTTING OFF ∞

"It turns out that an eerie type of chaos can lurk just behind a facade of order - and yet, deep inside the chaos lurks an even eerier type of order."

Douglas R. Hofstadter

∞ CUTTING OFF ∞

∞ CUTTING OFF ∞

First Day

"400 people applied. We interviewed 50. You eight are the best we saw."

I'm sat in the meeting room at a Royal Mail delivery office. It is late January 2012 and the weather is icy and snowy. I came home in July last year after seven months teaching English in Mexico. After travelling on and off for twenty years, I wasn't prepared for the drought that awaited me with regard to employment. I had applied for at least six jobs a week and got nowhere. Finally this one bore fruit. After five months on benefits I have landed a job as a postman. Online application followed by a face to face interview and then a security check. Me and the other seven successful applicants are facing the DOM, or Delivery Office Manager. Next to him is the Assistant DOM.

"You will all be partnered for the next week with experienced posties until we feel you are fit for working independently. Lance?" He looks my way and I raise my hand slightly. "The postie you're with has been with us for twenty years, he's a good bloke so listen to what he says."

He then breaks down the structure of what we've been employed to do. On part-time contracts we work five hours per day. The job description is "Postman/woman (with driving)" but he makes it quite clear that it will probably be months before we see the inside of a Royal Mail van as

11

∞ CUTTING OFF ∞

anything other than a passenger. We are the "floaters", the crew that come in later in the morning to clear up what's left. Due to needing to be trained up we will be in at 8.30am until independent. This will give our tutor posties time to do what's called the 'sorting' and then show us how to prepare the delivery.

The DOM waxes lyrical on the trust position that we have been given and how lucky we are. He then talks of how long Royal Mail has been in existence and the company reputation. Then he looks at his watch and to the Assistant DOM and then says brightly "OK, we need to get you lot out there. Good luck, I'll see you tomorrow."

We leave and head to the main floor of the delivery office. This is one massive room about the size of four football pitches. Over 100 people work in it. There's mainly posties but also what's called "cage staff" who handle the stuff that needs to be accounted for like Special Deliveries and the cash from the Packet Office downstairs plus van keys.

On the left hand side are three offices. One for the line managers, one for the DOM and another for the guy who handles the accounts and paperwork. The line manager's office is packed out at certain times of the day. Three computers shared by the Assistant DOM and the two supervisors. The DOM's is smaller, can be locked from the inside and has shutters. The accounts office is even tinier and the desk is a mess of papers and overtime sheets, spreadsheets and attendance forms. You can guarantee that at any time of the morning, between 6.30am and about 10 o'clock there'll be someone in there talking to the long suffering guy who sits in the well worn chair.

I'm introduced to my tutor, a short guy in his fifties named Gary with a big grey beard, grey hair and glasses. He smiles and shakes my hand warmly.

"Welcome to Royal Mail Lance, they told you everything?"

Stamina

When I started, in January 2012, it was mid winter in England and fucking cold. My tutor was great guy who showed me the ropes and was very good at the job, friendly and reassuring. As we were doing his Walk together it wasn't very strenuous and we were finished before the designated End of Shift.

Once I was let out on my own however things got more serious. My first solo Walk was in a rural area of the town, half housing estate, half country lanes and bordering the green belt separating the town from its neighbour a couple of miles away.

I'd cycle to the start point, about two miles away from the delivery office with one bag in the tray on my bike. Then I'd lock the bike up (a company rule) and deliver the first bag. Once that was finished I'd cycle up to the local newsagents where the Safe Drop was located and put the empty bag down (plus any letters or packets from people who hadn't been in when I'd knocked) and grab bag 2. This would be repeated until I'd finished and then I'd make my way back to the delivery office on the bicycle, with the empty bags either over either my shoulders or in the tray. Once back I'd pouch off and then go home.

Simple.

Reality was like a kick in the teeth however.

When I started as a postie, Amazon were still using

∞ CUTTING OFF ∞

Royal Mail for their deliveries and made up at least 40% of the packets we had to deliver. I thankfully missed the Christmas period as I started in January but days would sometimes see a mass of parcels to be sorted. Especially on my route as it was predominantly middle class and had a lot of people ordering stuff from both Amazon and Ebay. Back then I'd leave out anything I considered too big to take on a bicycle and at some point during the throwing up, a driver would come by and peruse what I'd left out.

Bloke who had the frame next to mine used to say, "If in doubt, leave it out" but all of us would chance it with something that was on the borders of 'reasonable size'. The lady driver who dealt with my end of town would look at the pile and grab what she considered acceptable, shoving other items back under the frame. This usually went something like:

"Morning. Right....taking that. Taking that. Taking that. Not taking that...or that...DEFINITELY NOT THAT. Taking that....".

Once I got to bundling up the Walk, I had to work out which packets could go in the bags. The ones I had could still be bulky, long or both and sometimes a separate trip out would be necessary just for packets. Not in itself a hardship but still a bum ache when minutes add up and my daily shift was five hours.

The golden days of postmen can be seen in drawings in children's books from the 1950s with smiling men in caps

∞ CUTTING OFF ∞

and smart uniforms, wearing a solitary satchel and waving to small children. The workload by the time I joined was a LOT more than that cheerful chap in Enid Blyton books used to have to do. It had increased over time and posties who'd been in for more than 20 years told me that back then, they had just a few packets each week, the majority of mail was letters and bills and by Saturday they were finished by about 11am at the latest unless they did Ghost Overtime.

Then we had the advent of the Internet and the reverse happened. By the end of the 2000s, most people were sending emails, not writing letters and online sales were through the roof. Also the advertising material, called Door To Doors, made up a big chunk of our daily deliveries. You know, that stuff for Specsavers, Pizza Hut or Subway. In my first couple of years you'd spend an hour or so on a Monday putting them into every single slot in your frame. Then you'd throw up your mail and only addresses that had actual mail going to them would have Door To Doors being taken out that day. Not long before I left, management changed this rule so that you had to do Door To Doors each day, regardless of whether there was anything else in their slots.

The Walks themselves are calculated by people whose job is solely to calculate Walks. They, in theory, work to some mathematical formulas and predictions based upon how long it will take to get there, how long the route

∞ CUTTING OFF ∞

should take, how much dead walking there will be and where the Safe Drop is. They are then meant to factor in meal and comfort breaks (taking a piss) and come up with a Walk that is do-able in the time a postie has at his or her disposal.

However...with time restraints, budget cuts, human error, not to mention the delivery offices potentially being fined for any mail not delivered each day, the powers-that-be would shave the Walks to the very limit of reasonableness and sometimes beyond. The definition of "reasonable" switched from something that could be done comfortably while walking along whistling and exchanging pleasantries with the public, to something that could only be done provided you focused your entire energy on it, didn't stop, and moved at (the very least) a fast walking pace.

DOMs and ADOMs I met during my time at the delivery office used to justify this by saying that the "old days" had been the posties having it easy and now was only that they were being asked to work to their contracts. When I pointed out that they'd had it "easy" for decades and that had therefore become an established "normality", it didn't cut any ice.

The Walk I had to start with was relatively compact with about fifteen roads on it plus a large retirement home. In total there was probably 300 to 400 addresses on it but not all of them required mail each day. The Walk itself was

∞ CUTTING OFF ∞

maybe three miles in total and in theory it should have been relatively easy. Something that wasn't factored in (and I didn't even consider until a knee specialist told me so, after I had an operation in 2015) was that the walking up and down people's driveways made a BIG difference to your daily mileage. Individually or even a couple of dozen addresses, it's nothing major. When you have hundreds per day it adds on the journey. The Occupational Health department told me years later (and long after the bikes had been scrapped) that the average distance a postie walked per day was around 8 to 10 miles, sometimes more.

Something I found very quickly was that my stamina was tested right from very early on. This in itself wasn't unexpected and was part of the job I'd signed up for. The job is physical and requires you to also concentrate and focus. In Spring or Summer it was lovely. Shorts on, no jacket, shades and some sunshine. In Autumn and Winter it felt like boot camp. I remember being physically tired to the point that climbing the stairs at the retirement home was a major pain in the arse. My shoulder hurt from where the bag strap was digging into it and when I had a heavy bag the ONLY thing that I looked forward to is that it could only get lighter as I moved forward. Also the multiple layers meant that you would sweat profusely unless it was very cold out and that again would affect your stamina. By the time I got to about ¾ of the way round the Walk, I'd be moving slower, my head down and just looking forward to finishing. Cycling home would be in itself a chore, even with no load to carry bar what I had to take back. Once I'd pouched off I'd feel grubby, tired and grumpy.

This wasn't the job's fault, it was just the way things were.

One thing that was NEVER factored into anything was that the colder or wetter the weather is then the more sluggishly you move. Your body slows down and you need to have the stamina of a trained soldier or athlete to overcompensate for that. When I raised this point (when challenged about why I was unable to finish a Walk in the rain that I could normally complete in dry weather) I was flatly told that I should simply walk a bit faster to warm up.

Something that I vividly recall is that at the back end of Walk 32 was a house with a heated porch. I would look forward to stepping into that little pocket of hot air for even ten seconds as it was a momentary relief from the cold. The first week on the job I came home on about the fourth day and fell asleep fully clothed on my bed. When it was just above freezing outside, I would eat a ridiculous amount of sweets each day, just to keep my blood sugar on an even keel.

It was about a year into my time as a postie that I had my stamina at a level where I could get home without feeling like I'd just woken up.

In the morning I'd eat porridge (slow burn energy) and

∞ CUTTING OFF ∞

make a fresh fruit smoothie (quick hit of natural sugars). Then I'd have two cups of strong, filter coffee with four sugars each (wakey, wakey). Out on the Walk I'd have a handful of sweets (lemon sherberts, humbugs or the like) and one or two snack bars. Then I'd pack a Scotch egg or get a sandwich filled with ham and cheese and take a flask of coffee (again with four sugars).

One thing about being a postie...it kept me fit.

∞ CUTTING OFF ∞

Floater

As a part time floater I had less work to do than the other posties in the depot. Most would start at six thirty and prep door-to-doors. At 6.45 there was sorting for at least an hour. After that then prep up letters, flats, parcels and do re-directions Then possibly helping on other people's Frames (latecomers, part timers, those off sick). Then maybe a smidgen more sorting and finally back onto their own frames for final prep and getting things squared away. Out the door by about 10am.

In January 2012, the looming beast that was privatisation was growing nearer but hadn't yet kicked in. However even then you could see that the workloads varied between "normal" and "WTF?!"

Most posties want to simply get in, get prepped, get out and get home. Being interrupted on Prep every so often by managers shouting "CAN WE HAVE YOU ALL BACK ON SORTING PLEASE?!!" tended to rile the majority. The depot I worked in was one of the bigger ones (I found out later its grade was a level 2, third from biggest). On my second day I heard a manager yell out for posties on the sorting frames, only for about thirty people to yell back:

"FUCK OFF!!!"

Beautiful thing was that, even though cursing (especially at Blue Meanies) was a suspendable offence, when this happened they couldn't pinpoint who'd said it

∞ CUTTING OFF ∞

due to the multitude of people so invariably they'd pretend they hadn't heard it.

A depot at six thirty in the morning is a chaotic place. The one I worked at would have around ten people stood around the potato sacks that were used to put people's parcels in. There were about fifty of these things, hanging off metal frames, secured with plastic hooks. Speed is the most precious thing in a postie's job and the packets would fly like hail stones as they were tossed from the yorks into the bags. This would usually take up to an hour, longer at Xmas and the result would be untidy heaps protruding like mole hills over the top of the bags.

Sequenced mail was stuff you received in boxes that was (theoretically) in the order that it would be thrown up into your frame. This made the job much easier as you simply had to work left to right, moving up until the box was empty. You could get up to ten of these, depending on the size of the Walk and what day of the week it was. Mondays were almost always light unless it was Christmas whereas Wednesdays were much bigger.

Beyond that you had non sequenced stuff that you had to simply drag out of the cubby holes in the sorting frames and put in yourself. Once you are used to the layout of a frame it's easy but can be frustrating if you are stood there like a kid with a piece of a jigsaw puzzle trying to find which slot fits.

After that you work your parcels in and any that require

a signature, you would place a While You Were Out docket in the slot and put the packet above it on the shelf at the top. The shelves were clearly designed in an era when parcel traffic was light, as invariably you'd overflow onto the next section, have stuff multi-stacked or even on the floor.

Finally you would go off to get your Specials which had to be signed for at all times, so the colleague in the Cage would give them to you and you'd sign to say you'd taken them, thereby assuming responsibility.

Bags were much sought after. Most guys I worked with would shove them behind the frame but then anyone lacking their own would simply come in and snaffle them. I saw some people take them home (permissible) or even padlock them to the frames (also permissible and funny if someone tried to take one and then found out they couldn't).

In the early days of my time as a postie we used bicycles. They were short, squat, yet reliable little things with a tray on the front. You were issued with a lock and a helmet (which you had to wear...at least while in site of the depot) and that was that. Only people in jobs that began a mile or more from the depot got vans, while those whose Walks started close to it were totally on foot. The bike was about the unsexiest cycle you could ever imagine but it had 3 gears making hills easier. You'd set off with one bag in the tray and get stuck into that from your designated start

∞ CUTTING OFF ∞

point. Then you'd go to the Safe Drop where a driver had left your other bags and take them one at a time until all were empty.

∞ CUTTING OFF ∞

Won't Take Long

As I was bundling up with my tutor on day three I heard the following ding dong in the next aisle. A line manager attempting to persuade a postie to take part of a cut-off out with him, from somebody else's Walk.

"But you can take it with you it won't take long."

"As I've just told you it won't take me any time at all because I'M NOT DOING IT!!!"

"But it will only take you twenty minutes and it's very easy."

"Yes, it's very easy in fact it's so fucking easy it won't take me even twenty minutes because I'M NOT DOING IT!!!"

"But you could do it on your way home."

"I could but I'm not going to."

"You could finish it really quickly you know, it wouldn't take you long."

"It won't take me any time at all, see I've already finished because...I'M NOT DOING IT!!!"

"It's very easy it won't take long."

"Yep. I agree, won't take me any time at all because (deep breath) I'M NOT FUCKING DOING IT!!!"

"But you could..."

"I could but I'm not going to."

"You won't take...."

"Won't take anything coz NOT DOING IT."

∞ CUTTING OFF ∞

"But it.."

"Oh for fuck's sake!!!"

The postie storms off while the manager stands there looking sheepish. After a few seconds he turns to another guy, still throwing up his Walk.

"Would you..."

Without even turning around the postie snaps "Don't even THINK about it."

Equipment

Royal Mail has lots of equipment. Lots and lots.

When I first went to the depot for my interview the place looked daunting.

There were mail bags and frames for the mail bags. There were big upright trolleys (that I later found out were called yorks) and there were huge frames that the posties put their mail into before going out. There were big boxes on huge long tables that were called sorting frames. There were loads of orange delivery bags and loads of boxes of stuff and if you went downstairs you had bicycles and vans and more yorks.

I remember standing outside the DOM's office waiting for my interview and it was about 8am. Everyone was still getting ready to go out and the noise was a constant hubbub of voices and the occasional barked request or order from a manager. Posties were moving around quickly (I later found out that time is of the essence) and absolutely no one bar those in the offices was seated. The whole thing looked chaotic. Scattered on the floor were rubber bands and the little paper labels that came with the boxes of mail. It resembled a redder version of those old photos of the stock exchange during trading.

The best thing that Royal Mail issues to its posties is their uniforms. While it's not the sexiest formal attire out there (less so since they moved from blue to red), it is

∞ CUTTING OFF ∞

functional and designed to keep you warm and dry. The only area that they DIDN'T skimp on was a postie's kit.

I was issued with a hi-viz storm coat, hi-viz waistcoat, fleece jacket, fingerless gloves, baseball cap, wooly hat, bicycle helmet, fisherman's hat, windcheater, waterproof trousers and ice cleats. On top of that I got to choose what type of shirt I wanted, polo T-shirt or a formal type (I opted for the former) and was given five of them, one for each working day of the week. Then I got a pair of shorts and two pairs of trousers. Most of this had the Royal Mail logo on it and was top quality gear.

The best bit though was the footwear. You got a pair of boots or shoes and a pair of trainers. The boots were Doctor Martens, Caterpillar or Magnum and the trainers were Caterpillar too. These would have cost at least a hundred quid a pair in the shops and it proved that the powers-that-be knew that healthy feet were fundamental for someone required to walk miles every day. You were entitled to two pairs a year.

Problems arose with the other stuff though.

When I started most of us were on bicycles. In an office at the back of the loading bay, facing the two freight elevators was a bloke named Chris and that was his workshop. He was the bicycle man and any problems you went to him. His workshop was always warm and he knew his stuff and was always friendly. Need some oil, see Chris. Need nuts and bolts tightening, Chris would do it. Need a new lock, Chris was your man.

Then we stopped using the bikes and they shipped them off to Ghana (as only with special permission could they be sold/ given away to citizens in the UK in case they had an accident and then sued Royal Mail) and Chris retired and his workshop was gutted and became empty and the only thing it was used for was charging PDAs from the wall sockets.

The trolleys we then had to use when we changed the methods came in two types. If you were on a van job you got a golf trolley thing. These collapsed so they could be stowed in the back of the vehicles and the newer delivery bags had reinforced loops to hang them on the sides of the trolley. Two at a time. Nice and simple. Problems arose when the fucking things broke (which would happen regularly) and after the first six months, finding one that wasn't faulty was like trying to find a fart in a Jacuzzi, especially for me as I came in at 10am as a Floater and most had already been nabbed.

Also the older bags couldn't be used with these as they didn't have the loops on them meaning you could spend up to fifteen minutes searching every frame in the delivery office for bags appropriate to the job in hand.

The bigger trolleys were the HCTs. These were big, red, double compartment things that had a lockable front and back section, a tray underneath and were meant to be the future of the business. The original ones were slightly

∞ CUTTING OFF ∞

smaller than what we called HCT2, and lacked the tray on the handlebars (with waterproof flap) that the later models had. In theory either a 1 or a 2 should have been able to hold not only the mail but also your lunch, water and your waterproof clothing plus any parcels you needed to bring back later on.

Truth was that the Walks became unmanageable due to being grossly underestimated with regard to how much was doable in the given shift periods. Time and again I'd see posties leaving the depot with HCTs that they couldn't close the lids on, and sometimes another bag of mail on the top. This was mainly caused by the drivers no longer taking responsibility for parcels off Walks and the posties having to do it themselves. Only Specials would go with the drivers due to the time restraints. Some twonk in an office somewhere had worked out that the parcels would be manageable along with the mail but didn't take into account that these things weren't fucking Tardises and only had a finite amount of space inside them.

What most of us used to do in order to get management to be sensible about all this, was to weigh the HCT on the huge scales at the back and refuse to take them out if they were even 1 kilo over the maximum permitted weight. Eventually this led to them getting drivers to take some of the parcel loads (or putting floaters on just packet runs, especially at Christmas).

The locks on the lids would break semi regularly and as

it was a disciplinary issue to leave mail unattended you had to flag it up to a manager who would then tell you to take it out anyway. If one side locked but the other didn't then it was useable as you just had to put anything valuable such as personal belongings or parcels in the other side.

The brakes would knacker with gleeful abandon and again, if one worked but the other didn't, they'd tell you it was OK to take it out.

There was a gap between the front and back panels in the middle of the HCT on the top. This would attract filth due to the rain that and also elastic bands that fell in. One time I took a pen and fished out the crap in there. It was utterly revolting and reminded me of digging up worms in the garden as a kid.

With the departure of Chris (and presumably all the other guys like him all over the UK) we had to rely on a company called ROMEC. They were the handymen for absolutely everything and they had three levels of grade on jobs. Immediate, Urgent and Normal. Someone getting stuck in one of the elevators would be an Immediate (apart from the time an unpopular manager on the night shift got stuck in one and they put it on an Urgent. Apparently he was in there for three hours wailing) but a faulty brake on a HCT was a Normal due to the amount of money an Immediate cost the company.

I remember once going into the delivery office and

∞ CUTTING OFF ∞

there wasn't one functioning HCT left in the entire building. There were however a total of five waiting for ROMEC to arrive and fix them.

The frames where we threw up the mail were antiquated and unsuitable for the job. From an era when mail was light and packets were sent on birthdays and Christmas, they had a roughly half inch gap for each address (unless it was a school, hospital or one known to get loads of letters) where you had to wedge in the mail. Separating each address was a plastic 'insert' that worked like a filing system with roughly 300 to 400 per frame, depending on the size of the Walk. One in about every ten was broken due to the mail being forced in and breaking the foot on the bottom of the insert. There were aeons old coffee and tea stains on the frames where some had been spilt and no one had been able to clean it without dismantling the entire thing. The paint was chipped and faded and they had the aura of stuff built in the 1950s. Sometimes you read stories in the press about old letters found from the late 19th or early 20th centuries in postal depots. Something that had got wedged between two filing cabinets or behind a frame and was only found decades later. In my depot we never got one that old but letters from the early 1990s turned up twice when the frames were unbolted and moved en masse one day.

Rubber bands are a necessary part of a postie's job. They hold the bundles together and without them you simply can't do your job. Something has to hold a bundle in one piece.

Every so often a big box of bands would arrive and be placed outside the managers' office. For a few days we'd just help ourselves but then it would run out and people would jealously guard the ones they had. Either putting them in the drawer on their frames (and woe betide anyone trying to "borrow" some without permission) or, less cautiously, in their bags.

I arrived several times for work and had to scrounge around for bands, getting yelled at by one guy for "stealing" off his mate on the next frame and feeling like a scavenger until I finally got enough to bundle up.

We also had security doors that, for obvious reasons, had codes to allow you to get in. The one leading down from the conference room was where the managers used to go for a smoke and was always working as it was the old fashioned tumbler system. The one that led from the dock to the main stairwell was a tumbler too but as most people hated the hassle of having to put down whatever they were doing to open it, it was almost permanently on the latch. Same for the one the other side near the downstairs toilets.

Behind the packet office was an electronic roll gate operated by a code you punched in from either side on keypads. This was almost permanently broken due to the amount of use it got day in and day out.

Dogs

When most people think of Postmen, they think of dogs as well. And the thing they think of primarily is that dogs and posties do NOT get on.

This is partially true but most of what you hear about the average pooch and a postman is exaggerated or even made up.

Dogs are, by their nature, territorial animals. They are loyal to whoever owns them and will protect their homes. They will usually bark or growl at strangers (or people they know but have at that moment failed to recognize) and in some cases may even lunge at those they feel are trying to invade their turf.

As my first job involved a lot of houses where the dogs were shut up inside, the most I'd ever usually hear was a muffled "woof" and the sound of paws on the hallway carpet. Sometimes when I rang the bell to deliver a parcel the door would open and the occupant would forget that Rex or Fido was behind them and the dog would run out to investigate. This never resulted in a bite but once or twice the mutt would run around me barking and its owner would assure me just how friendly it was as I stood there moving the delivery bag to cover my testicles and wondering if my tetanus shots were up to date.

One house on my first Walk of the job was on a terrace. When I put the mail through the letter box the dog that lived there would run up and tear the letters to pieces. This was a shock the first time but when I knocked to tell the owners their attitude was "meh!" and they suggested I leave any letters under the doormat. I pointed out that I couldn't do that due to the fact anyone walking past could take it so they shrugged again and said to just put it through the door.

Brilliant!

For the next six weeks (until I was placed on another Walk) I'd always look forward to that house as it was an opportunity to forget the cold and the wet for a minute or so while confetti was thrown around by an aggressive boxer, shaking its head and growling furiously as it shredded its owners' mail. I'd even put them through one at a time. Only thing missing was some popcorn.

In the US there are stories of mail men carrying tins of Mace to spray at aggressive mutts. In the UK the only advice Royal Mail would give us was to "rattle the gate and wait" if we were approaching a property that we knew or weren't sure had a dog in it. Any address with a dog deemed too dangerous would be marked on the relevant frame with an orange card (and in some depots, amusingly, a little sticker of a paw print) that either warned the postie to be careful or in extreme cases, meant the occupier had to come to the depot to get their mail.

One posh road on a Walk in the nicer part of town had a dog that used to stand in the driveway glaring at me and

∞ CUTTING OFF ∞

growl, snarl and lunge when I got close. However, it was tiny and I wasn't that arsed as I had sturdy boots on. When I left the dog would then follow me down the road, still growling and barking like all it wanted in the whole world was to have a good scrap.

One day I was in a particularly foul mood and when the dog followed me I just stood still and glared back at it. It continued to get closer, growling and snarling, until it was right by my feet. When I bent down towards it, it then simply rolled on its back and let me rub its belly.

In another part of town was a house with a couple of Westies. These are cute dogs by and large but one at this particular address clearly had a screw loose. The highlight of that Walk was when I delivered letters there. The lounge was next to the front door and the curtains were always open. Every time I turned up the Westies were asleep on the sofa, on their backs, contentedly dreaming of a nice juicy bone or whatever it is that dogs dream about. After the first time the dogs reacted, I had it down to a system.

I'd tiptoe up to the front door and gently lift the letterbox flap. Then I'd push the mail through and let the flap clang down. Within two seconds the larger Westie would wake up, look around to identify where the noise had come from, see me and then go utterly mental.

First thing it would do was to jump off the sofa and run round the back, coming back with a toy stuffed in its mouth (a different one each time) and, with its paws on the

∞ CUTTING OFF ∞

window sill, stand there growling and repeatedly bobbing its head...all the while staring me right in the face.

Next to it would be the other Westie, looking on and wagging its tail enthusiastically. I always imagined the dog was thinking:

"You! You again! You touched my door! WHAT have I told YOU about touching my door?! Well, you see this toy? The one in my mouth! Well I'm gonna stick it up your arse! RIGHT UP YOUR ARSE! You won't be able to sit down for a week mate! I'll teach you to touch my door!"

I further imagined that the other Westie was thinking: "Ooh you are so brave! I do love it when you shout at the Postman!"

The owner turned out to be a guy who drank in my local and one day he was there cleaning his car in the driveway when this performance happened. He chuckled and told me that the dog was called Rupert.

Somehow that made the whole thing even funnier.

Only time I was ever scared by a dog was when I rattled the gate, waited, and then walked in to hear the sound of running paws and growling. Bracing for a chomp on the leg, I was confronted by a large Alsation that simply ran in circles around me while barking its head off. Unsettling but nothing bad happened except my heart rate spiking.

There was a darker side to all this though.

One day I was on loan to a nearby delivery office and while in the middle of delivering mail to a block of flats, a

∞ CUTTING OFF ∞

woman rounded the corner holding a chicken. "Not something you see every day" I said smiling but she looked upset.

"My neighbour's dog just savaged it, it's dying. Would you mind wringing its neck for me, I can't do it?"

Not something you get asked normally so after a pause I replied "OK but not in front of you, could you go back in your house please?" She handed me the bird, which looked like it was about to fall asleep and said to put it in the green recyc bin when I'd finished. Across the passage was a neighbour who seemed concerned about the whole thing. As the door closed I tried to break the bird's neck but it wasn't like in the movies where they just twist and go. I think it died the first time I did this as I pulled as well as twisted. Sensation was like when you pop the bubbles on that plastic packing paper. After a couple of minutes I was satisfied it was dead and put it in the bin, then knocked on the door to ask if I could wash my hands.

As I scrubbed up the woman said that her neighbour had threatened to kill all her chickens with his dog and when that one had got into his garden he'd simply stood there laughing as his dog attacked it. I dried my hands and advised her to call the police, as it was criminal damage. She was still upset but agreed and thanked me for helping her.

Feeling mightily heavy after that I opened the door to find what could politely be described as a Chav holding a

Staffordshire Bull Terrier on a lead, talking to the neighbour who'd been watching as I'd euthanased the chicken. The neighbour looked up and said "Yeah, it wasn't dead. He had to ring its neck".

The Chav grinned and said "Yeah, my dog did that. Threw it around like a rag doll".

I just stood there in disbelief and then raised my hands, clapping very slowly and then said "Well done, you couple of fucking wankers!"

I walk off and make my way to the van, silence behind me. I see a guy getting into the car next to the van and after a brief conversation he tells me the Chav's name is Andy. As I get in the van, I take my phone and call the police. After the usual "Which service do you require?" intro I'm talking to the control room. I explain the situation and that the dog's owner was outside the house as I left and that I'm concerned he'll threaten or even attack the woman. As I'm talking I hear a tap on the side window and someone tries the door handle.

Now...being cynical, an ex cop and just slightly paranoid I ALWAYS hit the door lock with my elbow as I get in. It's a subconscious reflex and most of the time I don't know I've done it until I try to get out again. In central locking vehicles this will put the entire van into safe mode. Standing next to me is the Chav. "Hang on" I say to the operator and go "What the fuck do you want?"

"I want to talk to you"

∞ CUTTING OFF ∞

"Yeah, well I don't want to talk to you".

"I want to know what she said to you".

He walks off back behind the van and my common sense evaporates and I forget he's a stranger and has a big dog that likes to savage other animals. I get out, still holding the phone to my ear and walk after him, only then realizing that he's still got the Staffy on a lead.

"I know your name's Andy because a neighbour told me. Now do you want to tell me your surname to I can tell the police before they get here or do you want to simply fuck off?"

The operator then chips in with "Could you calm down please?"

Chav Andy looks confused and a little hurt but then says "I'm making a complaint about you to your company" and then walks away with his mutt.

∞ CUTTING OFF ∞

The Good, The Bad & The Ugly

Part of being a postie is, of course, meeting the public. Now the public come in three main types. The good, the bad and the ugly. Good ones are normal people who talk to you like a human being, may make pleasant small talk while you are on their doorstep or even leave you something on Halloween or at Christmas.

The bad are the moany cunts who seem to think they are still living in an era of the working class having to doff their caps to their betters. They will tell you that you're "late", moan that they were most definitely "in" when you left a While You Were Out card recently and generally behave like they are your only customer and your entire attention should be focused upon them, with a large helping of subservience and a side order of grovelling expected from you to help sweeten the deal.

The good people were about 90% of those I met while doing this job. Being a postie is hard work. It's monotonous, can be tiring and in unclement weather is beyond unpleasant. A smile or a kind word can really brighten your day (I was once nearly in tears after finding some Halloween candy on a windowsill with a note saying "For the postman, please help yourself" as I stood there soaking wet with numb fingers and toes, dreaming of a hot cup of coffee and a shower).

I have spent a lot of my life working with kids and as I

∞ CUTTING OFF ∞

write this book I recently qualified to teach children the self defence system of Krav Maga. I really like children and I used to say that if I got to see a baby, a puppy and a kitten on the same Walk then it wasn't a bad one.

Kids can be funny, especially as most of the little ones have seen or at least heard of the TV character Postman Pat. One day I left the HCT on the pavement and went to a posh row of apartments to deliver some stuff. When I got back a father was stood there with his little girl.

"It's a postman's buggy sweetheart he uses it for...oh here he is".

I smile and crouch down towards the kid "Hello there, what's your name then?"

She gets all shy and retreats behind her dad's leg, staring at me with wide eyes. He chuckles and says "It's alright Tabitha, you can talk to him".

I stand up and open the front flap of the trolley, dropping in a parcel from someone who wasn't in when I just knocked. "Want to see how my trolley works?" The little girl nods and her dad picks her up under the armpits so she can take a look inside. I point out the various compartments and the letters, all bundled up with elastic bands. Then I show her the bell on the left handlebar, the brakes and finally the lock. She is clearly curious and smiles the whole way through. As I finish up I reach for a While You Were Out card and whisper to her father "Can she read yet?" he shakes his head and I say to the kid "I'm a good friend of Postman Pat and he asked me to give this to you." She beams and takes it off me, smiling at her dad.

"What do you say Tabitha?"

"Ank oo".

He thanks me and shakes my hand, and they walk off with him saying "Aren't you lucky".

Another time I was going back to the delivery office, soaking wet and cold and in the normal bad mood that a rainy, cold shift can bring on. As I got to the bottom of town a couple of women from a pre-school I sometimes delivered mail to were pushing a big red cart with six tiny little kids in it, no more than about 3 years old. They were all dressed in wooly hats and tiny little scarves and gloves, with big eyes, watching the world going by. I stopped to watch them pass and couldn't help giggling when I saw the words "Bye Bye Buggy" emblazoned on the side of the thing. As they saw me watching them the women smiled and I said "That has DEFINITELY cheered me up".

One of them laughed and said "Good. Everyone wave at the postman". All of them then raised their little hands up and waved at me as they trundled past.

Beyond cute.

Other times you'd meet people who would like to have a chat and sometimes I even got invited in for a cup of tea. One old man was chatting to me on his driveway and said out of the blue "If you ever need to use the toilet, don't hesitate to knock on my door". This was like gold dust and

I made certain that a discreet note of this act of generosity was recorded in the log book for the Walk.

One time I was in the Packet Office and an old lady came in. She was ancient as hell but very chatty and was walking with a stick. As there was a queue I asked the people ahead of her if they'd mind if I served her first. Once I'd got her parcel she began chatting.

"Ooh, you're a nice young man. You remind me of my Sidney. Honest as the day was long my Sidney was. Been gone 20 years now, God rest his soul. I'm 91 you know. Still like to get about. Nice to see such a nice young man such as you. So many people have no manners these days."

Everyone in the queue is now giggling and I say "It's been a pleasure to serve you my love, you have a good day yeah. Is there anything else you need?"

"I'm fine thank you. My hip plays up in the cold you know. My Sidney used to drive me everywhere, God rest his soul".

Etc.

Bad customers were around too though.

On my first Walk were two roads with almost identical names. One was Old Miggleton Road and the other was Old Miggleton, a tiny village a mile further along. A driver took mail for the village as it was only about ten houses. From sorting, through throwing up to the actual delivery, occasionally mail for the village kept through into my Walk and I'd miss seeing the absence of "Road" at the end of the

∞ CUTTING OFF ∞

address. One arsehole took great exception to this and one day I turned around to find him stood behind me (after having followed me up the road) standing there silently, holding a letter up with the address facing me. I took my headphones out my ears and just glared back at him.

After around thirty seconds I went, "I don't speak Telepathy, what do you want?"

He looks uncomfortable and says "Wrong address".

"Oh? Really?! Well why didn't you say so. A thousand apologies, I'll get that sorted for you".

Another time I was delivering mail to a cul-de-sac on some vast housing estate when a woman emerged from her house holding a phone.

"Have you missed me?"

"No, just doing your neighbour first".

"Oh, I thought you'd missed me. I'm waiting for a packet".

I look in both bags that are slung either side of the golf trolley and there's nothing for her. However I had some oversize packets that wouldn't fit in the bags, that had I put in the back of the van for a Packet Run once I've finished all the letters and small parcels.

"Nothing I'm afraid. I've got some separate parcels in the van that I'll be doing later on".

"You're supposed to have it with you" she snaps at me.

Her tone and manner have just got right on my tits but I bite my tongue and continue.

∞ CUTTING OFF ∞

"Like I said I have other parcels in the..."

"You're supposed to have it with you. I can't wait all day".

"And I can't tailor my route to suit you!"

"WHAT DID YOU SAY?!"

I approach her to hand her her mail and she snaps "What's your name please?"

I ignore her, give her the letters and then walk off silently.

"I SAID WHAT'S YOUR NAME PLEASE?! RIGHT! I'm calling your depot right now."

She then puts the phone back to her ear and says "Did you hear what he said? Can't tailor his route to suit me!"

Later on it turned out her packet was in the van, way too big to fit in the bags. I went back fully expecting a row but the old cow wasn't in. I knocked on her neighbour's door. He took it and said "She had a right go at the postman earlier".

"I know. That was me. She always like that?"

He chuckles and nods while signing my PDA. "Yeah, she shouts at my kids for treading on her lawn".

Days later I found out she'd complained officially. She also lied and said that I'd sworn at her but the DOM took my word over hers and the incident was forgotten almost immediately.

Another time I walked up to a house just as a car pulled up outside. The driver was watching me silently, through

∞ CUTTING OFF ∞

beady eyes as I tried to get a flat packet through the letter box. After a few seconds she suddenly screamed "IF IT WON'T GO IN JUST LEAVE IT!"

I jump and turn around "What?!"

"You're doing that". She makes a see saw motion with her hands.

"First of all don't shout at me. Secondly if you don't like it raise an official complaint".

"So what's your name?"

"Mr. I'm Not Telling You".

The ugly were few and far between but there were a couple of them.

The town courts were on one of the Walks I covered. From the Magistrates up to the Crown court were in one big building. One day I met a delightful fellow who was on his way there.

Walking with a HCT and a guy aged about 17 wearing a pair of headphones was walking on a collision course towards me. He could politely be described as casually dressed, with a baseball cap, grubby jeans, hoody, and a strut like he's got a metronome in his hips. At the last moment he steps to one side and I nod acknowledgment and say "Thanks mate."

He takes one earphone out and goes "What?"

I take both my earphones out and repeat "Thanks mate."

He glares at me and then sneers "Thought you'd have

47

∞ CUTTING OFF ∞

moved out the way for me!"

After a pause I reply "Err...I'm the one pushing the big, heavy, hard-to-move-out-the-way thing."

"You fucking prick!"

"Charming, you have a good day yeah" (I go to move on).

He glares at me, steps a couple of feet back and then says "You wouldn't be smiling if I was to take a blade to you and wipe that smile off your face."

I look back and smile again then take some mail out of the front of the wagon. "Big scary guy like you, ooh! Wouldn't want to mess with you would I?" I slam the hatch.

"No you wouldn't, if I wanted to I could have you lying on the floor in 5 seconds flat."

He is WELL out of striking distance and has his hands jammed into his front pockets. His tone is flat and unthreatening and it's clear that he's simply monologuing a stream of threats that he's used times before.

I wave my hand at him. "Not talking to you any more, go away." I take a bundle of mail and go to move to the next house.

"What you say?"

"You deaf as well? Fuck off!"

"Seriously mate if I didn't have somewhere to be I'd lay you out right now." He walks back so I stand on the other side of the wagon and decide on a compromise between

∞ CUTTING OFF ∞

walking off and having to actually engage with the little shit.

"I'm bored of this. Tell you what...!" I put one earphone back in and hold the cable halfway up and pretend to press a button with my thumb. In my ear are AC/DC demanding to know Who Made Who?

"What you gonna call the old bill or something?"

I smile and hold up my hand for quiet and then pretend to have the following conversation:

"Voice activate number 5. (Pause). Hello, police please. (Longer pause). Hello mate, yes can I have police assistance to outside 23 Letsby Avenue. Male. About 17 years of age is threatening me and being verbally abusive. I'm a postman so I'm concerned about the integrity of the mail."

The Chav continues to just stare blankly at me.

"My name, (false laugh). No I can't tell you that as he's standing here listening to me. Ok, thanks. See you in 3."

I pretend to hang up and say brightly, "Whatever you're thinking of doing you've got about three minutes so be quick."

He steps back again and mumbles, "If I didn't have to be somewhere I'd just stand here and wait for them, I'm not afraid of the filth."

"Good for you, that's the spirit. You have a good day yeah."

He slopes off up the road.

∞ CUTTING OFF ∞

Another time there was a particularly unpleasant woman who lived in council accommodation and acted like the lady of the manor despite being on benefits. She blew hot and cold and would sometimes be very friendly and chatty and others a complete cow. One day she refused to sign for a parcel for her neighbour and then asked if I wouldn't leave her mail in her allocated box as the front had been ripped off. This was a reasonable request but officially I was supposed to so I said "That's fair enough. I am supposed to though. If you maybe leave a note on the box and I'll tell them at the depot that....."

Before I could finish she snapped "I'm not arguing with you about it" and marched back indoors.

I finished what I was doing and as I pulled the communal door to the apartments shut it closed with a loud bang. Not my intention, but shit happens.

As I got to the street there was an elderly couple standing near my trolley and the woman asked if I'd mind posting a letter for her.

"Well we don't normally but no problem my dear, I don't mind doing...."

"DO YOU MIND NOT SLAMMING THE FRONT DOOR LIKE THAT?!! THE BABY'S ASLEEP!"

I jump in shock and turn to find the gobby woman standing fuming in the driveway leading to her flat, still in her dressing gown and bunny rabbit slippers. The old couple look embarrassed and I feel my temper fraying.

∞ CUTTING OFF ∞

"I'm not talking to you, go away." I turn my back on her and resume my chat with the old couple.

"DON'T SLAM MY FUCKING DOOR LIKE THAT, I'M REPORTING YOU TO YOUR COMPANY!!"

She slams the communal gate harder than I shut the front door, presumably determined to make certain her baby stays awake. I lose my rag, and yell after her:

"Piss off you fucking silly cow!!!"

As I turn back to the old couple who are now silent with confusion and embarrassment, the gate creaks open again and I'm confronted with the sight of what I assume is the boyfriend. He has a baseball cap on, baggy shorts, and a large, faded tattoo on his neck. He's also got his right hand stuck to the depth of his wrist...down the front of his shorts.

"What'd you say?" he mumbles.

I take my earphones from around my neck and put them in my pocket and sigh "You ARE joking me?!"

"What'd you say? The baby's sleeping, don't slam the fucking door like that!!"

His atrocious missus then starts the predictable mantra.

"Leave it babe, babe...leave it...come inside babe! He's not worth it babe!"

"You mind not holding your dick when you're talking to me?!"

He moves closer, still with his hand shoved down his

∞ CUTTING OFF ∞

pants and I take one step back with my right foot and put my arms up left arm forward, right arm half extended, palms up.

"Back off, just stay away."

"Babe, come in. Leave it babe!"

"What you gonna do?!" he smirks, getting closer. When he makes contact with my left hand I shove him away.

"FUCK OFF!!!"

He backs off but continues making threats as he moves away towards the gate. "What you gonna do?"

"Seriously mate, just get lost. What YOU gonna do anyway? Wipe the hand you've had your cock in on me?"

He glares at me from the gate with his hand still cuddling his genitals and then mumbles something more about what I think I'm going to do then disappears.

I turn back to the old couple, who have their mouths open silently.

"Sorry you had to see that folks. More than happy to post your letter for you my love, you have a good day."

∞ CUTTING OFF ∞

Shorts

Most posties like to swaddle up in the bad weather. Scarves, jackets, fleeces, you name it. The weather in England is, in the main, wet and cold. When I started it wasn't uncommon for me to go out wearing a vest, Polo shirt, fleece and storm coat. This gave me the maneuverability of a medieval jousting knight but kept me toasty as I mooched about shoving stuff in letterboxes.

One guy in our delivery office used to wear shorts no matter what the weather. Rain, shine or snow you could guarantee that Jason would be in his shorts. And not Royal Mail issue shorts. Oh good heavens no! Jason would be in a pair of football shorts.

One morning I turned up at the depot to see posties walking away from it in droves. Management had decided to shut it due to the ice on the roads which, even while wearing cleats on our boots, was deemed too dangerous to work in due to slippage risk. We all got paid for an impromptu day off (after all, wasn't our fault we couldn't work) and came back the next day when it had thawed a bit.

The thing I remember most about this emergency closure (it only happened once in the nearly 4 years I was a postman) was that, stood outside the delivery office as I walked up, dressed like Ranulph Fiennes on an Arctic trek...was Jason in his shorts.

∞ CUTTING OFF ∞

He had a storm coat on but his legs were on display in a chill so ghastly that it felt like it was ripping into your very soul.

I looked at him and went "Seriously? Can you even have kids any more? Your nuts must be frozen solid".

He chuckled and went "It's better than trousers, trust me".

Months later I asked him if he was wearing shorts to prove a point (in some depots you'll get guys who have a bet to see who can wear shorts the longest, even into the frigid misery of an English winter). He then told me the logic of what he was doing and just why he was in shorts for the entire year.

When it rains or snows your trousers get wet and the fabric will remain damp as they are unable to dry unless the weather changes. Your legs are almost constantly moving due to the amount of walking posties do, and therefore are generating heat as they do so. By wearing shorts it means that the water can evaporate and you are actually warmer than wearing trousers as you don't have damp fabric against your skin to counteract the effects of the heat your legs generate when moving.

I tried this on a cold day a few weeks later. The wind nipped my legs for the first few minutes but, lo and behold, Jason was right. Well who'da thought it?

From that point on I was a shorts convert, and never wore long trousers again unless I was on duty in the Packet

∞ CUTTING OFF ∞

Office. My top half still resembled the Michelin Man and I wore thermal socks inside my Caterpillar boots in cold weather but shorts were the way to go.

This got curious looks off some members of the public and even the odd enquiry as to how I could POSSIBLY be in short pants in THIS weather. When faced with this I'd just preach the gospel of Jason and tell them about the relationship between movement and damp fabric and the generation of heat.

It also proved a hit amongst little old ladies.

One Walk I covered semi-regularly had a retirement home. On one occasion I walked through the lounge where a few old girls were sitting chatting.

"Ooh, look at him in his shorts. Mavis! Look at this"

"Oh yes, smashing legs he's got hasn't he Ethel".

"Hello young man, I could teach you a thing or two".

Etc.

∞ CUTTING OFF ∞

Security

In Royal Mail you are issued with an ID badge. This consists of a photo that they take of you on a digital camera on the premises and a week or so later, a printed card arrives with your name, age, position and the company logo on it.

You are meant to wear this at all times when on Royal Mail property, whether in uniform or not, and can be asked to show it if delivering mail to a cautious customer.

The delivery offices themselves have varying degrees of security depending on the size and how old they are. The one I was based at had a huge pair of folding doors across the main entrance with a padlock like Daenarys used in Game of Thrones to restrain her dragons. This was for deliveries and vehicles going out on delivery or collection and led directly to the Dock. There were three other doors to get in, all for pedestrians. Two had security codes and the other was a fire exit that could be opened with a key from outside.

In theory it was meant to be difficult, albeit not impossible, for intruders or unauthorised persons to gain entry. The loading dock had a barrier that could be raised and lowered (the kind you get in a car park) by whoever was on duty in the Packet Office who was able to make a visual assessment of whether doing so was prudent, by looking out of the window. Anyone wishing to gain entrance on foot was meant to turn up at the Packet Office, introduce themselves to the staff and then be signed in via a log book (after showing ID), given a temporary 'Visitor' badge and then escorted to wherever they needed to go.

We were told to challenge any and all people we saw in the depot that we didn't recognize and ask them for ID. This once led to the wonderful scenario of a VERY high-level management meeting in the conference room. Lots of blokes in expensive suits with titles like National Director for Deliveries. We had our Work Time Learning meeting after they finished and criss crossed in the corridor. I vividly recall seeing a veteran postie stand in one manager's way and ask politely to see his ID.

Some mail (such as Specials) had to be tracked every step of the way from when first taken to a post office, right up to when it was signed for. They couldn't be left out of your sight once you had them, unless securely locked in a van or in your HCT.

Vehicles had to be locked at all times if you weren't in them (a couple of guys were fired for leaving the keys in the ignition and the engine running when doing deliveries) and back when we used bicycles you had to lock them up when doing Loops.

HCTs came with bicycle locks and were to be attached to something like a lamppost or sign if you stepped away from them.

Self explanatory and common sense.

∞ CUTTING OFF ∞

However the reality was depressingly different.

The only actual thing that worked 100% of the time was the huge concertina gate with the dragon padlock. Once closed and locked it would take a tank to get through it. Once it was open though....well.

The car park guillotine thingy was usually left up as the amount of vans that needed to get in and out from 8am to about 10 meant that raising and lowering it constantly was an arse ache for whoever was in the Packet Office (and the drivers didn't like to be kept waiting).

Some local businesses had agreements with Royal Mail that they could bring their post directly to the depot in what was a Rough Sack and hand it over, where it would be sorted. This cut out the middle man and saved time. They were meant to go into the Packet Office to do this but many would simply walk right into the loading bay (a breach of Christ knows how many Health & Safety rules) and put the sacks on the dock. This wasn't commented on by anyone when it happened, and there was one guy who'd actually reverse his car in and then take two or three sacks out the boot before driving out again.

Management would still tell us in Work Time Learning that you had to be a member of Royal Mail staff to be on the loading dock and that you HAD to be wearing hi-viz clothing if you were. One day a new Director level guy was appointed who decided to test our depot by attempting to get in without ID. He walked up to the Packet Office and

∞ CUTTING OFF ∞

whoever was in there just waved him past. He then identified himself, gave the staff member who'd let him in a right bollocking and sent official communication nationally that the rules were now to be obeyed.

A day or so later I saw a woman walk in and place her bag on the dock. No high-viz. No ID on display. Clearly a civilian. I approached her, introduced myself and asked that in future if she could please report to the Packet Office as she wasn't allowed on the dock or in the premises at all. The conversation then went like this:

Woman (with fixed smile): "I've always done this".

Me: "Yes but I'm afraid we're not allowing people in any more. I'm sorry if that inconveniences you but if you wouldn't mind checking in at the Packet Office in future and leaving your stuff there".

Woman (still with a fixed smile): "I'm a customer and I think you're being rude".

Me (trying to keep my temper): "I'm within my rights to simply ask you to leave and then escort you out if you don't go willingly. I tell you what let's go to the Packet Office and I'll get them to let you know that I'm not winding you up".

We approach the Packet Office and the two women in there back up my story that this is a management directive and not just me being a jobsworth. I later found out that the customer had been making funny faces behind my back while I was talking to my colleagues.

On Saturdays the Packet Office closed earlier than

∞ CUTTING OFF ∞

normal and, as it was unfair to turn people away at the closing time who were already in the queue, at ten minutes to closing we'd lock the door to the office and the queue would move to the walkway inside the loading bay that we used to get into the office itself. Again a huge breach of protocol as it meant you had unauthorized people in the secure area but hey.

The doors on the sides were secure enough. One was rarely used by posties anyway as it led to the management offices and the conference room. The other was a roll gate that was constantly breaking down. It was meant to be used for bringing in HCTs, yorks and in my early days the bicycles. When it broke they had to get ROMEC out on an Immediate as it left the delivery office vulnerable. In the years I was there I think this bastard thing was broken around 50% of the time.

As you moved from the loading dock to the main stairs that led to the sorting room and main floor, there were other security doors with tumbler code locks. These were invariably propped open and in one door's case, usually broken.

I first noticed the difference in the security between depots when I dropped a van off at the mechanics at another delivery office. In full uniform and wearing ID I walked in to the main area to look for the toilet and was immediately accosted by a concerned manager who hadn't recognized me and demanded to know who I was.

The Packet Office

In every delivery office, even the tiny little ones, you have a packet or callers' office. This is where parcels and letters are taken to if you weren't in when the postie tried to deliver them. The majority are just bog standard packets in one vast section. Oversized stuff is kept on a separate cabinet of shelves and Specials, Tracked & Signed Fors are in another bit. Also loitering around are surcharged items and anything intercepted by Customs at the international borders for not paying enough tax.

Most times people would turn up with a red & white While You Were Out card that had been pushed through their letterbox and queue up until it was their turn to be served.

In the Packet Office you will get usually one member of staff in the early mornings and two in the busier times from lunchtime to close. At Christmas there can be up to four people in there, all busy nearly all the time.

When I started the Packet Office was inaccessible to posties and they had to hand their returned items through a hatch. This was later abandoned as it took too fucking long in busy periods. Instead they would enter and place their Specials in a mini york in the middle of the room while leaving normal packets, Tracked and Signed Fors in big yorks outside which the office staff would retrieve at regular intervals and then process. Letters also had to be

∞ CUTTING OFF ∞

handed in due to their squashable and tearable properties.

Another thing was that engineers working for British Gas would have the items they needed for their day's work shipped in recyclable plastic boxes to the packet office. Whoever was in first to open up would match the items with a four or five sheet itinerary and later on the guys would turn up for their gear.

In theory this was all manageable and simple. But true to form Royal Mail found a way to cock everything up.

For a start the main packets were in alphabetical order. This meant that if something hadn't been filed correctly then you could spend up to 30 minutes trying to find it. This happened semi-regularly, especially at Xmas and it was annoying for customers and embarrassing for us to have to search for ages only to have to turn people away empty handed.

Another thing they did was disconnect the phone in that office so we could only make internal calls to upstairs. Christ alone knows why they did this but it meant we were unable to call people back to say we'd found their missing items without traipsing up to the managers' office at some point.

To really push things out beyond any semblance of normality though, one of the line managers passed along a directive that if people turned up with a card that had their address on it but was in someone else's name at that address and not their own, then they had to have ID for the

∞ CUTTING OFF ∞

other person as well as themselves.

The logic behind this was that people might be "spying" on sons or daughters or spouses. That, quite frankly, was not our problem but we obeyed this for a week or two, which resulted in one bloke screaming at me that I was a "FUCKING JOBSWORTH!" and threats against other people. The other rule she invoked was that if someone had two items at the packet office but had only brought one WYWO card along...then you couldn't give them the other item, only mark it for delivery the next day or get the person to go home and then come all the way back again.

Finally the whole thing was quietly dropped and normality resumed.

ID was the biggest bum ache though. The original cards said you needed to bring ID but didn't flag it up loudly and clearly. Later versions of the cards had "PLEASE BRING ID" in big letters on the front and back of the card, in the middle of not one but two red circles each. Some people would bring inappropriate ID such as letters with address but no name and others would be rude if you refused to then give them their item.

Christmas was always hectic. Parcel volume went up by four to five HUNDRED percent and yorks would be erected in the loading bay, in around the second week of December to cope with the extra items. One godsend was that Amazon eventually stopped using Royal Mail for their parcels and did their own deliveries. This took such a

∞ CUTTING OFF ∞

chunk off the workload that we were all relieved.

At the busiest times the queues of people would be out the doorway and up the street. We would shout every so often "Specials need ID", or "Anything dated today won't have been processed yet" or the old chestnut "Blue and white cards are from the Post Office, not us. You need to go across the street". You could guarantee that every time you did this at least one person would sheepishly leave the queue in silence.

The bit the public stood in to wait was tatty looking, with faded, torn posters on the walls and even a ceiling panel missing. In Autumn the leaves would blow in from outside and collect in the room. The entire atmosphere was one that incited depression and anger (but was ironically cosier on the staff side of the counter).

The only time there was any sense of joy was Xmas when, despite the extra work, we'd have a laugh with both each other and the public and share cakes and chocolates. December 2013 a Mrs Christmas came in to pick up a Tracked item, telling me "don't give up the day job" when I made the obvious joke. Later we had two Mrs Shepherds arrive and a Mr Santha. I was wondering if Fate would throw us a Mrs Arguing With Relatives on Boxing Day, but no such luck.

Before I left they radically overhauled the whole thing with the phone being released once more, a computer with internet access being brought in, and EVERY item being

∞ CUTTING OFF ∞

given a unique identification number on a sticker meaning it could be tracked straight away. Just after I left they also gave the waiting room a new lick of paint, replaced the knackered ceiling panel and made the whole thing slightly cheerier.

Wonders will never cease.

Vans

One of the essential tools of the Royal Mail is its vans. They are bright red with the company logo on the sides and are recognizable the world over. They come in different shapes and sizes but the backbone of the fleet are the little ones, commonly referred to as "Escort vans". They usually run on diesel, they are reliable, they have enough storage in the back for most Walks and they get you from A to B (and sometimes to C). The required tyre pressure is thoughtfully displayed just above the wheel arches in little yellow print, and on the front and back will be a number to identify it.

The pictures you'll see on promotional material will invariably show a shiny, almost sparkling vehicle, surrounded by its equally bright brethren, that are glinting in the sunlight. If a postie is also in the photo it will show him or her in a crisp, freshly ironed uniform smiling in anticipation of an enjoyable ride in such a wonderful, four wheeled machine.

When I applied for the job back in 2011, the blurb said that it was "Postman (with driving)" however we were told on day 1 that we would almost certainly be walking or using bikes for the main part of our shifts and any van use would be rare.

Jealous of those who got at least temporary shelter from the British elements it was only when I actually got to drive one of the things that I realised most are basically petri dishes on wheels.

For a start there was only one dedicated mechanics centre in the entire Delivery Sector. That was in a Band 9 depot about 16 miles away run by four blokes who were permanently wearing overalls and didn't suffer fools gladly. If a van went wrong to the point that it couldn't be used, then a mechanic would drive out at the next available opportunity (usually the next working day) to take a look at it. Anything lower on the scale (i.e. the van can still move) then you had to drive it to the mechanics yourself. This resulted in TWO vans driving 16 miles with the faulty one driven by one postie and his ride home driven by another. This also applied when you needed to pick it up again.

The other thing was that the vans were invariably pooled, with hardly anyone having dibs on a specific vehicle. I heard posties talk about vans being personally assigned back in the Golden Days but the only guys I knew who got to use the same one regularly were the guy who drove the tail-lift, and those who did the parcel runs, particularly the lad doing the "By 9am" Special Deliveries. This lack of consistency meant that vans accumulated other people's garbage like a beach at Tipton in July.

Rubber bands accumulated like ants around a jar of honey, in the footwells, in the glove box and ALWAYS around the gear stick. With them being such an essential part of a postie's tool box, they had to be put somewhere

∞ CUTTING OFF ∞

and most guys (myself included) would stow them wherever was convenient at the time. Problems only arose when you then forgot (or couldn't be arsed) to take them with you when you finished your shift. Some gear sticks were like exhibits in a Turner Prize exhibition, with dozens and dozens of bands wrapped around them, wobbling like a misshapen pile of caramel jelly. While you could use these yourself if you needed, the ones on the floor had usually been there a while and were like something you'd drag up from the ocean bed. Weather in the UK leans towards the rainy side of things for most of the year, meaning that footwells could have up to half an inch of what looked like cold, milky tea in them where people had repeatedly got in and out wearing wet boots and clothing.

Another issue was people leaving their own crap in there. If you wanted to play 'I Spy With My Little Eye' then you could place a safe bet on getting a view of an empty sandwich box, an almost empty bag of crisps and one or two chocolate bar wrappers crunched up into the map pockets, under the seats or on the floor. Almost as prolific were empty plastic bottles, and pie or pasty wrappers. After that you could find a few low denomination coins amongst the brown water in the footwells and maybe a long forgotten hi-viz waistcoat jammed behind one of the two chairs. Tissues, newspapers, even half eaten food. It wasn't nice.

Seatbelt laws in England are pretty tight and the

internal rules of Royal Mail meant that you had to wear one at all times. The vehicles would flash a warning (usually both audible and a light on the dashboard) to tell you if you hadn't put it on. With some parcel runs involving jumping in and out of the vehicle every 50 metres or less, a lot of people simply couldn't be bothered. Numerous times you would retrieve a van from the car park at the start of your shift to find the safety belt across the seat and the locking clip in place, meaning your predecessor had sat on it without wearing it for their shift, to avoid having the warning light irritating them.

It was a requirement in the job that you had to do at least a cursory check in your van EVERY time you took it out. A log book was handed to you with your keys and you were meant to take a few minutes looking at tyre pressures, windscreen wash, oil, radiator etc. This meant if you ticked and signed the space in the book for that day to affirm everything was Jim Dandy, then you would be in trouble if something later turned up that you hadn't flagged up. This could be a busted headlight or the interior being messy. Due to the state of the majority of the fleet, management tried to invoke a rule that any mess not noted in the log book would result in the postie who last had the van being obliged to clean it. A great idea in practice, I can just imagine two or three high level managers and the DSM giving each other high fives around a table after thinking that one up. It was however grossly unfair as

∞ CUTTING OFF ∞

some guys would simply get in, not see the mess (as they'd seen it countless times before and were immune to it by then), and return the van. It wasn't their van or even a van they regularly used and invoking "last one who touched it, owns it" was childish.

A couple of time I overheard conversations that sounded like this:

Manager: "Ah John, glad I found you. Van 36! (sucks air through teeth). That's in a hell of a state, rubbish everywhere. Says in the log book you drove it yesterday. I'm afraid you'll have to tidy it up".

John (continuing to prep his Walk and not turning around): "Fuck off!"

Manager (slightly taken aback): "Err...excuse me?! You can't speak to me like that! If you look here you didn't....(proffers log book opened at last entry).

John (still prepping Walk): "Fuck off, I ain't touching the fucking thing. And if you ask me again I'll get the Union involved".

(Manager walks away red faced while the sound of posties sniggering can be heard in all the rows near to where the conversation just took place).

Another time I wrote "Interior of van full of crap that isn't mine" on two consecutive days in the Notes section of the log book to forestall any attempts to make me clean it up. On day 3 a line manager asked for a quiet word in the office. Once I sat down she handed me a photocopy of the

∞ CUTTING OFF ∞

notes I'd made and then said theatrically:

"I find that word offensive".

(I look at the text quizzically for a few moments): "What word...'van'?"

"Don't be facetious".

(I look again) "Interior?"

"Stop being silly".

(I look a third time and then equally as theatrically hold up my hands) "Oh, 'crap'? That isn't a swear word, hasn't been for about 30 years, you can even hear it in Disney movies these days".

(Manager looks momentarily flummoxed but decides to try and retain the moral high ground) "Well, I find it offensive".

"And I find it offensive to be given a van that looks like Worzel Gummidge has been dossing in it."

After a few minutes of this we agreed that I would no longer use PG rated swearing and would instead describe the state of any vans I would given using proper words. Next day I wrote "Interior overflowing with a veritable assortment of detritus that was not placed there by my own hands".

Keys issued for the vans were meant to have a fuel card on them in a little holder. This meant, theoretically, that when you did your daily check, you would notice that some selfish bastard had left the tank running on fumes and then drive up to the local petrol station to fill it up.

∞ CUTTING OFF ∞

However there were only a limited number of the cards to go around meaning that you sometimes would have to traipse back upstairs and ask for one. On a few occasions I had to wait up to 15 minutes then be told that there weren't any left. As there was no petty cash on site bar what was kept in the Packet Office and Royal Mail wouldn't approve you paying yourself and then claiming it back, you simply had to wait until one DID turn up. The cards were also authorized to pay for oil and a car wash. At the tail end of one shift I filled up with diesel and then spent about 10 minutes getting the van a cheap spruce. It looked like something from Mad Max when I was given it and came out looking a few shades shinier. When my line manager found out that I'd done this he was annoyed that I'd spent 10 whole minutes cleaning the van when I could have been trying to get a couple of parcels delivered.

One thing that could get you suspended or even fired was leaving the van unlocked while you were delivering, or putting Special Deliveries in places where they could be reached or even seen when you weren't there (such as on the passenger seat not covered up). A couple of guys I knew were dismissed for this after getting stung by IB agents on random checks.

The "alerts" these things had in them were sometimes welcome (the seat belt one) but others could get right on your tits. Newer vans had some posh woman's voice saying loudly "Please apply the hand brake before leaving the vehicle" while others would sound a piercing klaxon if you shifted the gear stick into reverse to inform Joe Public that you were about to go backwards.

Provided you actually held a valid, full, UK driving licence you could drive a Royal Mail vehicle BUT they weren't supposed to let you unless you had done a thing called Change Over. This was a short trip out with a certified Royal Mail driving examiner, who would affirm that you weren't liable to drive it into a brick wall or leave the hand brake off when parked on a 1:3 incline.

Six months after I started I was driving Royal Mail vehicles and only did Change Over when I stepped up to the bigger boy's club of Transit vans. There were a few raised eyebrows when I mentioned this to management years later. The joys of what's called Grandfather Rights on a UK licence means that anyone who passed their car test before 2001 gets to drive big vans, moderate sized trucks, mini buses (and even steamrollers) without further examination. This meant I could drive bigger Royal Mail machines with just the Change Over. The test took about 3 hours with me and the instructor was top notch and said that a Transit was different in that it "loves" to be in 3rd gear and to rely mainly on wing mirrors when reversing or turning due to the greatly reduced visibility and blind spots.

∞ CUTTING OFF ∞

The Relationship Project

Royal Mail made the big step in 2013 to actually find out how the posties felt about work, managers and what life was like as an OPG. This was a big thing, with about national four depots getting involved, and the one I was at being one of them.

A big, black metal box appeared outside the DOM's office with a note on it saying that if we wished to participate in the Relationship Project then to put our names in and after a set date, they'd pull a few out and those people would get to attend.

As it meant time off work that you couldn't then be penalized for, I was up for it. We were promised that a national level director would be attending, along with a national level CWU rep. There would be about 10 of us and everyone would get to say how they felt without fear of reprisal. Once we'd said our pieces, the DOM or another manager could then attend to be given our feedback and respond to it.

Sounded fab.

And for a couple of weeks it nearly was.

My name got pulled out with others and the following Tuesday (they held this on a light day) at 9am we met in the big conference room facing the church. A female director was there and she was friendly and reassuring, saying that the whole purpose of this was to get feedback.

∞ CUTTING OFF ∞

To allow us to voice any concerns or gripes we might have and then have them discussed in a civilized fashion. She added that normally it could be difficult to present your opinions to senior staff so this was our opportunity and it was up to us if we took it.

We started things off relatively restrained and then a very vocal postie, been in the job 28 years and vocal of his dislike of management began to state what he perceived to be the flaws in the current system.

And he got most of it right.

He pointed out that management bark orders at the posties. That they could be rude and even swear yet posties were told off or sometimes suspended for the same behaviour. He mentioned that one new manager had completely ignored him outside the depot when he'd said hello to him and he thought that was ignorant. He said that an acting manager that absolutely nobody could stand (mainly because he was acting up in his own depot, never a sensible thing to do) had for some reason been the acting DOM the week before... and when the actual DOM had been questioned as to why the reply came back that "It was because no one else wanted to do it".

He went on to say that managers were inconsistent, used bullying tactics to get Walks completed and did not practice what they preached. When he'd finished the rest of us chipped in and the general picture wasn't pretty.

For some strange reason, when the previous DOM had

left to go to Afghanistan with the RAF (as a reservist he'd been called up) we had two DOMs for the transitional phase of handover and for a while after. One was a short guy with glasses and the other was a huge, hulking bloke who said very little. Together they'd walk around the delivery office and occasionally go up to people and ask what they were doing. It reminded me of a loan shark taking his enforcer out to collect on debts.

Normally management would only interact with posties when it was initiated by the posties themselves or when necessary. Random "chats" were not something OPGs were used to. Also the questions tended to be along the lines of "What are you doing?" which, to be fair, was to give them a clearer picture of how the posties did what they did and not for any reasons of blame laying or criticism. Problem is that if you have people that are used to being left alone, then any and all intrusion by senior staff into their working environment is likely to piss them off.

One of the expressions used was that "managers hunt in packs" referring to the impromptu visits, and the perceived rudeness of the big, silent DOM who came across as grumpy and anti-social. It was further added to the list of complaints that managers needed to listen more to what posties said and take their suggestions on board.

After about half an hour of this, the shorter DOM then came in to hear what we'd said. Our input was anonymous, known only to the people who'd been in the room as we'd said it. He listened in silence as the director read out the remarks and then countered a few of the points. He conceded that yes, the managers should take ideas on board and he would prepare a method for that to happen. He agreed further that if managers were using foul language then that was unacceptable and posties had every right to call them on it to their faces. He did however disagree strongly with accusations of bullying and said that some of the posties seemed to think that if they said they wanted to cut off then that meant it was the end of the discussion, whereas the agreement with the union was that a compromise needed to be reached.

We wrapped things up and made our way back to the floor to get ready to go out. Our Walks had been 95% finished for us, as they knew we were being paid to attend the Relationship Project and they couldn't force us to stay over.

After bundling up I put my head in the DOM's office to say I thought I'd be able to finish without the dreaded Cut Off. The DOM looked up and said "Managers hunt in packs eh Lance?" and the expression on his face suggested he was quite hurt by the remark.

After a pause I replied "I don't agree with that sentiment but I can see why they feel that way. It's a question of perspective. If you're used to being on your tod and then two guys come up and demand to know what you're doing...it's going to annoy you. Especially if one is chatty and the other is a big hulking bloke who hardly says a word".

He smiled and nods then says "OK".

Within the following weeks there were marginal improvements in the relationship with the managers. They became a little less acerbic and would take ideas on board (or at least pretend to) without simply dismissing them. The silent, big DOM turned out to be a nice bloke who was simply shy and didn't find it easy to talk to people. The veteran postie who had criticized him in our first meeting, told us at a later one that he'd had a private chat with the guy and his opinion had changed once told this.

For a few weeks, maybe even a month, things looked a little brighter. And then the national director stopped attending and so did the national CWU rep. The managers went back to giving orders and not asking for our input, and we were left with just one DOM, not two (the big guy, who did continue to make an effort to be amenable).

The last meeting I attended there was only about four posties and the once high level attendance from senior leaders was nowhere to be seen.

Like all good ideas in Royal Mail, it faltered and faded away due to lack of interest.

Cutting Off

When I got to Royal Mail they were gearing up to privatization (while simultaneously denying that it was an inevitability) and the one thing I noticed above everything else was that the equipment we had to deal with our deliveries wasn't big enough for them.

Back in the day it all presumably had been but by 2012 it was like trying to bail out a sinking boat with a teacup.

The frames were too small for the volume of packets and letters. The Packet Office wasn't big enough for the amount of stuff it had to hold (Christmas would see yorks being placed in the docks where the bicycles used to be stored, in alphabetical order). The vans sometimes weren't even big enough to hold the amount of stuff you had to deliver, necessitating two trips. The delivery bags would sometimes split from being overfilled and most worrying of all, the HCTs weren't always big enough for the amount of mail they had to contain (even though they were supposedly the Next Generation of postal badassery).

When I started there was an expression used quite a lot called Cutting Off. Managers reacted to it like they were hearing fingernails being screeched down a blackboard while posties would talk about it and the union would discuss it. It turned out that it was something you were entitled to do but controversial in the extreme to anyone in a blue & orange waistcoat.

∞ CUTTING OFF ∞

It basically meant that you weren't going to finish your job and were cutting off the part of the Walk that you believed you wouldn't have time for. Years ago this was virtually unheard of but in the era of privatization, it happened more and more frequently until eventually Walks were created solely from the Cut Offs of other, less palatable Walks.

It was a union agreement with the company that posties could not be forced to finish their Walks. If an OPG thought the job in hand was too much they were required to flag it up to a line manager who would then speak to the postie and an agreement would then be reached (kind of like haggling, but with mail).

This in theory was a civilized way of dealing with the issue.

In reality it was far from it.

When I started I spent a week being tutored and was then released as competent to work on my own. As a part timer and Floater, I was meant to come in at 10am to find whatever Walk I was on completely thrown up and ready to go. The ONLY thing I was meant to have to do was bundle up, get my Specials and make my way out.

What actually happened was that for the first four weeks I could come in to find the Walk half or three quarters ready and big piles of mail on the frame, where someone had been dealing with it but had then left to do something else. As a newbie I was unaware of the rules

∞ CUTTING OFF ∞

governing this type of thing and when the line managers told me that I should throw it up myself and "It'll only take you 20 minutes" I didn't question it. It was all new and I went along, eager to please and to make a good impression.

They'd then lament me leaving later than I was meant to and argue with me if I tried to claim overtime the following day (OT was meant to be agreed BEFORE you left the delivery office), even though the alternative would have been to bring mail back with me.

The basic problem was that there was way too much mail and not enough time or people to deal with it with the system as it stood. Management would NEVER admit they were wrong (and this attitude got worse the higher you went up the food chain) and it was only after months of a problem being criticized that a different method of dealing with it would be tried.

Once they phased out the bicycles and shipped them off to Africa, they tried a new thing called Shared Van jobs.

This was an utterly brilliant idea that one van would take two Walks with two posties in it. They would go to a designated start point and then 'loop' off to their respective deliveries, meeting back at the van to get the next bits and so on.

What anyone with half a brain could see through, was that this relied on having people who could work at the same speed, with roughly the same amount of mail each, and who were as experienced as each other. It also relied on both of them knowing their Walks as well as each other.

When this started they put only the most experienced posties on Walks they believed would prove (as they put it) "a bit of a challenge". Within three weeks the posties were constantly stating that they were unable to deal with the workloads and management were constantly arguing with them for the sin of cutting off.

One day the DOM called me into his office and said that he'd personally selected me and a woman called Arat, to take one of these controversial Shared Van jobs and give it a go. He made a point of stressing that he considered us the best two people from our intake and wanted to know what we made of things. Reality was that they wanted other people to try the jobs to see if they really were as bad as the veterans claimed. And what better way to do that than by getting newbies to take them on for a bit?

The next day me and Arat came in at 9am to bundle up (for once the Walks had been fully prepared as they wanted to judge how long it took us without the normal delays due to stuff not being prepped in time). We were out by 10 o'clock and there was 16 full bags of mail in the back, 8 each. There was about 30 packets of varying sizes and about 5 Specials. We got stuck in, not taking a lunch break (just scoffing our sandwiches and some coffee while sat in the van parked up) and got the whole lot finished.

The next day the DOM said brightly "What time did you

finish then?"

"5 o'clock".

His face fell. This had been a Tuesday, a supposedly light day...and his two 'best' newbies had taken longer than the veterans. Taking off the fact that we didn't know the Walks plus experience and stamina factors, you're looking at roughly the same amount of time to do the work. We did this for two weeks until they quietly moved us back onto other jobs.

When they had calculated the jobs they did it as if the mail was being delivered by a robot. We heard rumours of some shadowy person who was called in to recalculate the routes whenever they needed changing and that whoever it was used algorithms and mathematics in their equations.

What it most probably was, was some arsehole trying to cut corners and impress his or her boss.

The Walks were planned by how much time it should take to walk to each address. This was then used to work out how many addresses should be on each Walk. However it didn't take into account some very basic truths.

The main one being that posties are only human beings and tire like other human beings. No one I met in this job was a former Olympic athlete and while the role keeps you fit, you will not be able to move at the same speed by the end of your Walk as you did at the beginning of it, especially if its pissing down with rain in February.

Another point was that the little seconds that would be

wasted on certain addresses all added up to minutes which became up to an hour or more on longer jobs. That house with the dog where you had to 'rattle the gate & wait'. That block of flats where you had to ring two or three bells before someone let you in. That woman who was never in so you had to leave a 'While You Were out' card. It all added up.

They didn't factor in what are charmingly called comfort breaks either. Shops usually let you use their staff toilets or at least point you in the direction of places that would. If you were lucky they'd be a pub or a public toilet on or near the route. However some estates didn't have any shops and on four or five occasions I remember, with my bladder screaming, knocking on some random person's door to ask if I could use their loo. This is embarrassing in the extreme, especially for a grown man. I was always super polite, pointing out that there were no shops nearby and it was perfectly fine if they didn't want to let me. No one ever said no but I hated doing it. Ironically some shops didn't like you to use their toilets and did refuse. You could guarantee they got their mail last of the Walk forever after that, possibly with footprints on it.

You were also entitled to a lunch break but management would encourage you to take half your meal relief at the beginning of your shift and half at the end to avoid having to pause midway through a Walk. This worked for full timers as they were in by 6.30am and could

∞ CUTTING OFF ∞

take a thirty minute break at half nine before going out at 10.

For part timers it didn't work as we were only meant to be in for about an hour at the most before heading out.

The maximum distance a HCT was meant to be taken from the depot was one mile. This was taken to ludicrous extremes on one poor sod's Walk who had his furthest address exactly one mile from the depot. It also necessitated a shit load of dead walking due to the way his Walk was spread out. As he kept cutting off that bit they eventually unofficially let him do it except on really light days and gave it to me or another Floater to take out. Later on it became part of the coping mechanism called the 'A' jobs.

Shared van jobs sometimes became farcical when you had one postie who couldn't drive, meaning he or she relied on their partner. This situation became even funnier if there was only one set of keys available for a van as they had to try and anticipate who would finish their Loop first so the non driver could sit in the van and wait for the other guy. The funny factor went up to eleven if you had both the above points...and it was a rainy day.

Christmas was even worse. With the triple fold increase in deliveries management still refused to see the elephant in the room, and would expect people to finish on time without cutting off. To be magnanimous they'd take a bunch of parcels off the Walk and give them to a driver.

∞ CUTTING OFF ∞

One time I remember two guys gleefully scanning a total of SEVENTEEN Tracked parcels to take with them. There was no way they were going to finish without incurring some serious overtime (which neither was prepared to do) but the managers just wanted them out the door so that, for a short while at least, the delivery office was free of outgoing mail.

It all came down to a question of perspective. We knew the Walks were undoable. Management knew that if we didn't do it then they had to (shit rolls uphill in Royal Mail). So they'd try bullying, coercion, threats of retraining or even pleading to get Walks taken and jobs completed.

One Walk I did required being driven out to it, being dropped off and then, once you'd finished, pushing the HCT back to the depot. All fine in theory but the journey back was 40 minutes, if going at a brisk pace. When I was asked the next day why I'd brought mail back AGAIN I mentioned this fact and the manager speaking to me tried to work in other factors to make out it had little to no relevance. He told me I chatted too much while prepping. That I was probably faffing about on the Walk. That maybe I needed retraining. He also mentioned the dreaded Wilful Delay. I told him to fuck off and went to see the DOM and the subject was never brought up again.

I genuinely didn't think things could become any more chaotic...and then I became a Duty Manager.

Acting Up

During the Relationship Project I had had a quiet word with the Director who attended, asking her if there were any vacancies for managers. I'd been wanting to apply for some time, due to the increased pay and the fact that it meant mainly staying indoors. The vacancies were advertised a couple of times a year but, true to Royal Mail ineptitude, you had to log on to your company email to see this (as the vacancies were internal promotions due to the 'acting' status of the role) and only managers had access to the computers unless you asked specifically to use one. Also I wasn't even on the system for emails or intranet access so couldn't get in anyway. I'd missed one window of opportunity so made certain I asked her the first chance I got.

She was chatty and appeared pleased that I'd asked her, taking my name and phone number and, after a brief talk, even adding "We're always looking for people like you".

The next day my phone rang while I was out delivering and it was her, saying that she'd spoken to the DSM and while the window had closed a week ago, she'd told him to put me on the list anyway and give me an interview.

Great news.

I kept this quiet from my colleagues, aware of the piss taking and possible resentment this might generate. Within a week I got called in for an interview with my own

∞ CUTTING OFF ∞

DOM and the DOM of a nearby depot. We did this in the big conference room at one end of the big table. They were friendly and offered me a tea or coffee, chatting about my motivation for wanting to do the job and then asking me questions about how I'd handle certain hypothetical situations. After about half an hour we shook hands and they said they'd let me know.

On the Friday I got summoned to the DOM's office to hear that my interview had been a success and that on the following Monday I'd be heading to a Band 9 delivery office 16 miles away to begin as a Duty Manager.

I was in hog's heaven!

He wished me well and then chuckled saying, "You know you've had a complaint made against you?"

I didn't and was vaguely worried so asked what it was about but he said he didn't know then added "Martin was killing himself laughing yesterday. Was going through the complaints off the system and got to that one. Was shouting 'Hey boss! You know that bloke you just passed for manager?!'"

"Do I need to worry about this?"

He shrugs and smiles then says "No it's OK, we killed it".

Turned out it was the woman who I'd told I couldn't tailor my route to suit her.

I was handed a still-warm print out of what a Duty Manager's role was within the company and he wished me

∞ CUTTING OFF ∞

well. Once I got home after my shift ended I read the sheets thoroughly. The job description was that Royal Mail needed a pool of trained managers to act up when needed to and that it was necessary to have staff willing to don the blue & orange waistcoat. The usual blurb about being proud of working for Royal Mail and the responsibilities the job entailed was also in there, along with a brief note that Duty managers would only be needed when the situation required them. This last line was something that would come back months later to slap me in the face. I found out that it also slapped a few other guys too.

I didn't have a car back then so made a few phone calls and within half a day had an old Seat Arosa that was reliable enough to get me from A to B and cost under a grand.

I sorted out a nice suit and polished my shoes, trembling with anticipation of the new role I was about to take on.

Biggest shock was the change in start time. I lived a seven or eight minute walk from the depot where I was a postie so used to get out of bed around 9 o'clock every morning to start at 10. The new place had a 6am kick off, meaning I was out of my pit at 5 at the very latest.

When I turned up the other managers were already there. Two new guys like me, an already established Duty Manager who'd been acting up a couple of months and three full time, substantive managers. The DOM hadn't got

∞ CUTTING OFF ∞

in yet and after brief introductions we were asked to jump straight in, as the depot was busy, even at 6.10am.

Nervous as hell me and the two other newbies were shepherded around by the two monther, shown the various places and tasks that needed to be done. Having been a Floater for 18 months and usually coming in when most people had already gone out, it was eye opening to see just how complex the structure was and how many people were involved. This delivery office was big, being a Band 9, and in one room off to the side of the main area were four huge sorting machines. Still working at them when we came in were a team of six women who'd been there all night and were about to knock off. We were briefly introduced and they told us how the machines worked. The machines were worth about 250 thousand pounds each meaning there was one million quid of hardware in the one room. They were apparently quite complex contraptions and rarely broke down but had to be maintained properly.

Around this room were various yorks with a wall containing ones dedicated to specific Walks, where the Tracked and Signed For parcels would be placed later on for the posties to take. On another side was a big space for empty yorks which would open up to enable stacking in the same principle as supermarket trolleys but on a bigger scale.

Off to the side was a long room full of metal frames where rough sacks hung. This was the parcel sorting room where posties would be designated to work. This was one job that had to be kept in check, as the sacks would fill up quickly and you occasionally had the fairly amusing sight of posties continuing to fling packets at an overflowing sack, as it wasn't their job to empty, only to fill.

Back in the main room was a vast collection of frames where you had about fifty to sixty Walks. Near to that was what could best be described as the world's largest bookshelf, where unsequenced mail would be placed in designated spots for specific Walks. The slots were box shaped, with a top, bottom and two sides but no front and back. They ran about twenty along by five or six deep. To prevent the mail from sliding out the other side, elastic bungee chords ran from the top to the bottom of the frames down each column. You had to keep checking on these as again they filled up pretty quickly and take them to the relevant frames.

Off to one side was the Cage, where a bloke named Albert handed out van keys, Special Deliveries and PDAs. Next to that was a room used for storage and further down was the Packet Office. Leading off from all of this was a corridor that led to a huge staff canteen and above that were offices and meeting rooms.

The place was BIG.

Me and the other two new guys had a chat. One was Adam the other Rory. Both were like me, posties who'd been interviewed the week before and got the job on the

∞ CUTTING OFF ∞

Friday. Both were nervous like I was and when we were taken up to the lady in charge of giving out uniforms she gave us the badges of office, the Manager waistcoats. Blue and orange with "MANAGER" on the back. Rory mumbled something about not wanting to wear his on the shop floor in case it looked like he was being arrogant. I pointed out that we were there as managers and were probably going to be disliked on sight anyway, so what did it matter?

When we got back down the DOM had arrived and he invited us in for a chat.

He was a big bloke named Peter, reassuring and quietly spoken. His substantive grade was level 4 and he'd worked as a line manager like us before acting up as the DOM, starting about six months ago. He said to come to him if we needed anything and that the other managers would help us if we got stuck or wanted advice.

Something that appeared odd at the time was that while Peter was a substantive 4, one of the line managers helping him was a substantive 3, a higher grade. Weeks later when I asked about this Peter said that it was because the DSM had said that the depot needed an experienced hand to help out and this guy was effectively an ADOM, while Peter was still in charge.

Around eight thirty we had a staff meeting in the canteen (with only half the posties, the others kept on sorting and throwing up, then they swapped) and Peter introduced us to everyone, telling them that we'd be

∞ CUTTING OFF ∞

knocking about and to not be surprised if they saw us regularly.

This was a reassuring first day. Being eased in to things and a helping hand here and there. When I came back the following morning it was just coming up to 6am and only a few people were in the delivery office. Within a few minutes the shift started and the place began to fill up and the work began.

The usual routine was that from 6 to about 8 it would be almost non stop. The depot was so big that there was a shed load of mail and packets to be sorted and things had to be kept running smoothly. The plastic boxes that were used for mail, flats and Door to Doors had to be stacked up so as not to get in the way. There were dozens and dozens of these things and they had to be slotted into one another like Lego, stacked up on a york which was then strapped up and taken into the room with the sorting machines and pushed to one side, ready to be collected by a driver later in the morning.

The mail in the sorting frames was a constant pain in the arse as you absolutely had to keep on top of it. The bungee ropes on the back (normally) held the letters in but every few minutes you had to do a check to see if the boxes were full. At peak sorting times it could take less than five minutes for an empty box to fill up.

In the parcel sorting room it was cramped and busy. By the time I finished at Royal Mail, they were using mini

93

yorks to hold parcels, a much more efficient method. Back in 2013 you had big metal frames separated into squares. On each square was four hooks at the corner and from that you hung what was called a Rough Sack, like you'd put potatoes in, to hold the packets. Posties would then get a york of parcels and throw them into the sacks. Experienced guys would know just from looking at an address which Walk it belonged to. The yorks were marked A, B or C which referred to which bit their parcels were intended for. Once full the bag would be taken off the frame, a new one put in its place and the full one then taken and left on the sorting frame of the relevant Walk.

Something I had expected but which happened very quickly was the fact that most posties simply don't like managers. A couple of times while I was taking full sacks off the frames a parcel would bounce off my arm that someone had thrown, who would then grin and go "Sorry, didn't see you there".

Another time at another depot I noticed a full sack of packets, detached it and then lugged it over to the Walk it belonged to. The postie was at his frame, chatting to his neighbour. I put the bag down.

"Here's your packets".

He glances at me quickly then says "I'm not ready for them yet, can you go and put them back please?"

He isn't even looking at me, there's no reasonable reason for this request and as I've never been at this depot

∞ CUTTING OFF ∞

before, chances are that he's simply trying it on.

I reply "No" and then walk off.

He blusters in indignation and then shouts "CAN YOU GO AND PUT THEM BACK PLEASE?!!"

Another line manager then steps in to sort it and later on both her and the DOM told me that that guy was the union rep, he's a bit of a wanker and was indeed trying it on as he liked to see if he can intimidate new managers. The DOM added that I'd handled it correctly as it is up to me to decide where the bag goes not him.

Once the main sorting had been done we'd then go to the individual frames and check everything was being dealt with correctly. The depot I 'made my bones' in had a total of seven managers, including the DOM plus Albert in the cage who was a supervisor. Even with this many people you had to keep your eye on the ball. There were staggered start times for some of the staff and that meant Walks had to be prepped and thrown up before they got in, or at least started so they could continue once they clocked on. On several occasions me and the other Duty managers and the substantives too, would be stood at frames trying to get Walks thrown up before the postie assigned to it came in, or the Walk had to be absorbed.

Absorption was one of the biggest bones of contention amongst the posties that I ever experienced. Basically it meant that a Walk would be broken up into small chunks and those chunks then given to various posties to deliver

95

∞ CUTTING OFF ∞

along with their normal stuff but at no extra pay. This was deemed fair by management who'd worked out that it was doable in the time of an average shift. The union had also signed off on it. If a Walk wasn't ready by the time the posties were ready to go however, it was unreasonable to expect them to hang on while it was prepared. The only alternatives in that case were that it was offered on overtime, the managers did it or someone drove the Absorption out to where the posties were so they could do it.

Van keys and Specials weren't given out until a specific time and this again was staggered, with Albert handing out the gear at a predetermined hour while a queue of about twenty guys stood impatiently outside the Cage.

It took about a week to get used to the rhythm of the depot and to keep on top of just how chaotic this whole thing was now that I'd joined the Dark Side.

Being A Manager

The bottom line with being a manager, whether you are a temporary level 4 or a DOM is that most posties think you're a cunt and the ones that don't are usually merely tolerant of your existence and any interaction they have with you.

The delivery office I was first sent to as a Duty Manager had a lot of people in it who were related. The union rep's daughter worked there. There were three or four married couples and one or two mothers and sons. As a result of this there was a kind of community amongst the posties that usually worked well. Only problem was that the managers were obliged to interact with them and some of the things we were asked to do did nothing except piss off the posties.

For a start it was a Health & Safety rule that the brakes on yorks had to be applied at ALL times while the york was stationery or unattended. With time being of the essence for deliveries, most posties had their own way of doing things and this meant cutting corners. I never saw anybody do anything deliberately dangerous but it is easy to forget basics, especially when you're busy and/ or when you are not used to being hauled up for it.

We were told that we were to ask people to apply the brake on their yorks and to apply it ourselves on ones that

∞ CUTTING OFF ∞

were unattended or stationery. The reaction this got was predictable with anything from raised eyebrows to a barked "HAVE YOU GOT NOTHING FUCKING BETTER TO DO?!!"

The only time that karma kicked in was when two posties were loading and just after I asked them to put the brake on the york, the whole thing overbalanced, tipped off the lip of the loading bay and smacked into the back of the van. The DOM made them both watch a video presentation on safety at work and fill out a Near Miss form.

I could totally understand why this annoyed people and it would have got on my tits if I was on the receiving end of it. Then again, we were told to do it and it was common sense.

Biggest thing we were told to clamp down on was people not wearing hi-viz vests when on duty. Due to the fact that everything moved so fast and you had around forty company vehicles in the car park at one time, a hi-viz was a Health & Safety must. We used to stop people from going out if they didn't have one on and I was once give the unenviable task of standing outside as people left and calling them on this.

Overtime was something a lot of people didn't want to do any more and it took a good relationship with posties to persuade people to stay on for extra deliveries. One day it was especially light for mail and some genius told me and another Duty Manager to stand by the entrance with a

∞ CUTTING OFF ∞

clipboard and stop anyone coming back early. If they'd claimed overtime the previous day we were to amend it by how early they'd come back. I pointed out this was going to gain us no friends and would result in absolutely no one offering their services to deal with cut-offs for the foreseeable future...but they still made us do it.

The weirdest thing the depot had though was the processing of stool samples for the hospital up the road.

An arrangement that beggars belief was that people would take a shit, then get a sample of it and place it in an envelope and post it to Royal Mail where it would then be sent on to the hospital to be scanned for signs of bowel cancer. This was meant to be a tiny swab, placed in a plastic bag and then in a jiffy envelope. The envelopes were also meant to be kept separate from normal mail (for obvious reasons) and collected separately, as well as sorted in a separate room.

However at least once a week we'd get at least one that had sneaked into the main chunk of letters and more than twice I was confronted by the sight an envelope with a skid mark on it.

There was even the urban legend of some berk who'd taken a dump in the envelope, rather than just taking a swab.

The processing of all this biohazardous, stomach churning filth was done on an old, wooden, wheeled trolley and the only nod to hygiene was that the posties doing it wore surgical gloves.

Once an envelope got into a sorting machine and ruptured, spattering the conveyor belt with cack. The whole thing had to be shut down for three hours while they cleaned it thoroughly.

I am not making any of this up.

Another thing that was farcical was the state of the car park and the loading bay. The staggered times for disembarking were set up to avoid too much of a crush but it still looked like the Omaha beach landings. To really push things beyond the realm of stupidity, we also had a huge, hydraulic garbage van arrive every Wednesday to empty the bins. He wasn't supposed to get there until about 10am, when in theory most people would have gone. He was another time conscious guy though, and if he was early he would just back in with his warning alarms telling us that "this vehicle is reversing" sometimes mere inches from the vans and people trying to load their mail. How nothing got damaged and no one got at least a toe run over was a miracle. Complaints to the company on the phone resulted in him arriving at the appropriate time for about two weeks and then simply turning up when he felt like it again.

Another thing we did was Huddles.

This was a great idea that meant important information didn't have to result in everyone stopping work to hear it. Managers would approach one end of a row of frames and

∞ CUTTING OFF ∞

ask for the attention of everyone up to a certain Walk, usually no more than about twenty people. You'd tell them what they needed to know, ask if there were any questions and then move on to the next group.

Simple.

Problems arose for various reasons though, the main one being that posties didn't like to have to stop working.

One time I was doing a Huddle and the guy on the Walk opposite where I was standing had his back to me and was continuing to throw up his mail. Everyone else had had to stop work and I didn't really like speaking to his back.

"Excuse me, I need to talk to you".

"I can hear you", the guy replies, without stopping.

"Do you mind turning round when I'm talking to you?"

"RIGHT!"

He slams the mail down on his frame and storms off. I tell everyone what they need to know and then approach the union rep. Staff are entitled to have someone present if a manager wants to speak to them about anything other than their delivery and this, in theory, could be a disciplinary issue. I tell the union rep what's happened and ask him if he wants to be there when I speak to the guy. He smiled and replied "Thanks for asking but it's up to him. Speak to him and if he wants me there let me know".

The guy is now back on his frame and I walk up. He ignores me but looks mightily pissed off.

"Can I talk to you?" I ask him.

∞ CUTTING OFF ∞

"I don't think so, I think you said everything you needed to".

"Why did you walk off like that?"

"Because you spoke to me like I was a child".

"OK, if that's how it came across then I'm sorry. Everyone else had to stop what they were doing and listen, I thought it was unfair if you were allowed to keep working AND you had your back to me. If you thought I was being condescending it wasn't intentional. I'm sorry you took it that way".

I extend my hand and he looks surprised but shakes it and nods silently. As I shake his hand I say "Just because I've got blue shoulders doesn't mean I'm going to try and bully you".

From that point on me and this guy weren't exactly best mates but we did get on a lot better and he was always amicable towards me. I later found out that his surprise was because managers never usually apologised for anything.

Another time I had a Huddle with a group on another row and was telling them about the fact that that car park across the road that we used for private cars due to ours being tiny, was only to be entered after a certain time each morning. As I was talking a postie aged about 20 and covered in tattoos turned to his neighbour and said casually "So what if I want to park there and the guy won't let me and I say 'fuck you, you cunt'".

∞ CUTTING OFF ∞

I tail off in mid sentence and just look at him. He catches my expression, raises his hand palm up and goes "Oh, sorry".

"Seriously? Right to my face!"

"Wasn't to your face I wasn't talking to you"

Swearing at Royal Mail was a big no-no.

Foul language was meant to be a zero tolerance policy. It was normally ignored provided it was just banter between people and managers could at least pretend that there presence wasn't detected when a 'fuck', 'shit' or even a 'cunt' was uttered. Swearing AT someone however was disciplinary and the only thing that was stopping this from going into the DOM's office was that the guy had simply used foul language while talking, it wasn't directed at me or anyone else.

However I am now in the awkward position of not being able to ignore it as he did it in front of me and he knows that I heard him.

We finish the Huddle and people move back to their frames. I approach the guy and say "Come on" motioning that we should step to one side.

Immediately the union sub rep steps up and links her arm through his like an overprotective mother hen and says:

"He's a good boy, he works very hard".

"Err...that's not up for debate".

The guy continues to throw up his mail and says "I said

I'm sorry".

The sub rep is still hanging on to him and tuts again, saying "I've heard managers swear".

"Yes but you've not heard ME swear. You've got a choice. This can be a 'Don't Do It Again' piece of friendly advice or we can take it to the DOM, it's your decision".

He huffs in protest, puts down his mail and we step to one side. The sub rep listens to every word as I tell him his language was inappropriate and he shouldn't do it again. I then point out that he said "the c-word" and in front of female staff.

He shrugs and says "Don't make out the c-word is worse than any other swear word".

I realise I'm going to lose this one unless I take it up to a formal level, which I had already promised not to do so I let him go back. As he walks off the sub rep says "A manager swore in front of me the other day, no one said anything".

"Fine, tell me who it was and I'll tell the DOM".

(Pause) "No, it's alright. I'm just letting you know, that's all".

One guy I worked with at this depot was a Team Leader named Carl. He was a postie with certain supervisory privileges and unfortunately this had gone right to his head. One day I was sat in the managers' office and he said brightly:

"You're a very lucky boy because of some of the changes

∞ CUTTING OFF ∞

I've been working on".

I look at him and ask "How old do you think I am?"

"Errr..about 32".

"Go up".

"35".

"Keep going".

He keeps guessing wrong so I ask him how old he is and he replies "42".

"Same age as me so I'm a very lucky 'man' but carry on, what were you telling me?"

His condescending attitude extended to other posties as well. He was an OPG grade who would sometimes be excused duties to work on projects (along with his girlfriend who did the same work) for the delivery office. This was merely an irritation until one day I was on the phone to another delivery office, trying to scrounge a van to borrow. I was on hold while that depot's DOM went to see if they had a spare vehicle. Carl was talking to his girlfriend and she said "They've told me I have to go out on delivery today".

Carl replied "You can't. You're helping me". He then gestures to me and another Duty Manager sat next to me and says "They should get a manager to do it, they do fuck all".

"OI!" I yell at him.

"Oh, sorry...err, do nothing".

I'm about to follow up on this when the guy comes back

∞ CUTTING OFF ∞

on the other end of the phone and all I can do is glare at Carl.

Afterwards I spoke to the other manager who said he was offended too. We had a quiet word with Peter the DOM who called Carl into his office and apparently told him we couldn't be spoken to like that and he was in the wrong. Half an hour later I saw him on the shop floor.

"Hey Lance".

"Yeah?"

He jerks his head "Come here a minute".

"Excuse me?"

"Come here a minute?" He jerks his head again.

"You want to talk to me, walk to where I'm standing".

He mooches over and a manager from another depot who's overheard this then stands midway between us, pretending to look at the frame he's next to.

Carl looks around then says "I'd just like to say if you've got a problem with me that you say it to my face next time".

"Had I not been on the phone I would have ripped you a new one for that. You know as well as me that a postie speaking to a manager like that on the shop floor would have been suspended on the spot".

He shrugs and goes "Yeah, true but you're not above me you know".

Truth is that I am, as are all Duty managers but pointing that out isn't going to defuse this so I don't argue

∞ CUTTING OFF ∞

the point.

"You were completely out of order and you shouldn't have spoken like that. Let's just leave it at that".

The other manager who's still pretending to look at the frame then pipes up "Come on lads, not on the shop floor".

Carl mooches off and I shake my head. The other manager told me a few days later that he thought we were going to come to blows over this, which was why he'd stood in between us. I replied that while I was annoyed I wasn't about to commit career suicide by lashing out.

Further Adventures in Management

As I moved through the role of a Duty Manager I saw a side of the business that, while interesting (in the same way a multi vehicle pile up is interesting) was also depressing. What became clear very quickly was that the system couldn't cope with what it had to deal with.

The basic "grunt" work was something that we could bear. With everyone pulling together and 'all hands to the pumps' each morning would see a deluge of mail and packets and door to doors and flats get sorted into chunks of labour, that would then be split up and organised. It was satisfying to see, after 3 or 4 hours that the mountains of mail had become ordered, filed and were ready to go out. As the posties left the depot, me and the other managers would finally take a tea break, going next door to the café or the newsagent down the road for some snacks and feel that we'd achieved something.

Then of course, we'd have to go back to work taking out the cut offs, filling out the information for the second DODR report and finding out if anything had been left behind.

After a few days I got to know the mechanics in the motor shop, on the other side of the loading bay. They were all in their mid twenties to early thirties and knew

∞ CUTTING OFF ∞

their jobs very well. Permanently in overalls, they were efficient yet didn't suffer fools and would get work done properly and in the time they said they would.

After a few weeks at that depot I was moved to a Band 9 in another town. This delivery office was even bigger, with not only a DOM but two ADOMs and about six line managers. It had about forty, mainly new, small vans in the car park and resembled a factory at peak times due to how busy it was.

Every morning one of the jobs handed out was that two posties would be dispatched to the mechanics to pick up any mended vehicles that needed collecting or to drop off any that were in need of repair. It was usually the same two guys who were asked to do this and as the whole trip didn't normally take more than about 90 minutes, it was done at about 7.30 in the morning to get them there for 8 o'clock when the mechanics opened and back for 9am so they could bundle up their Walks and get out on delivery without hanging around.

One day a van was sent over and the guy who'd taken it said to me, laughing, as he got back "That one was a bit messy".

I didn't think anything further of it until the phone rang two hours later in the office. It was Brett, the chief mechanic.

"Lance? Hi it's Brett at the auto shop. That van you sent over this morning. We're not touching it. It's fucking

∞ CUTTING OFF ∞

disgusting. I'll fix the engine problem as I only have to go under the hood for that, but the interior stuff...no way. Get it cleaned up".

The van had been filthy and I'd actually filled three or four old Tesco bags with what I'd dragged out of the footwells and map pockets, mainly so it could actually be sat in without someone squashing into old garbage. There had been a quarter eaten beef lattice behind the driver's seat and even some old cheese with fluffy mould on it. I found out who the van belonged to and went to find the postie.

Expecting to find some old, smelly, unkempt wretch I was surprised that the guy was about 25, clean shaven and even had a gelled hairdo and a clean T-shirt. I asked him for a chat and we sat in a small meeting room off to the side of the managers' office.

I explained the situation and asked why the van was so disgusting.

The postie shrugged and went "Just kind of got that way".

"What's your own car like?"

He shrugs again and says "I know what you're getting at, it's not like that. My own car's OK".

"When it gets to the point where people who work with oil and grease all day won't touch it...you know it's gone too far. I'm not going to lecture you about this but you've got a choice. We can either discipline you over this or you can clean it yourself BUT you won't get paid for that".

He opts for the second option, the van was collected the next morning and when his shift ended he spent a total of two and a half hours cleaning it out. By the time he'd finished there were eleven bags of crap including old food and rubber bands. He was given Cif and some rags and wiped the surfaces with it. When I came to check, it still wasn't perfect but was satisfactory for a work vehicle. Mechanics took it the next day without further comment.

One of the most frustrating things about being a manager was that things didn't happen the way they were meant to.

While I was meant to have a basic level of access to the company intranet, like all Royal Mail employees, it turned out that I didn't and had to apply to the IT department, based in Sheffield. This in itself shouldn't have been difficult. However as I was an acting manager I had to get the manager I was assigned to back at what was known as my home depot to endorse the application. The guy was on holiday for two weeks and this couldn't' be done by anyone else. This meant that for weeks I had to use someone else's ID to login to management bits of the system or simply wait until someone else could do tasks that I should have been able to.

Another thing was ID cards. They had various bonus features, one of which was the fact that they could be used to open the security doors at the newer depots by swiping them through a magnetic reader. However they needed to be assigned to the relevant delivery office, which had to be done by the IT department. After about a week at one depot my card was assigned to it.

Hooray! Hooray!

Only problem was that it then couldn't be used to open the doors at any other depot without revoking the authorisation at that depot and I moved on again within three weeks and it was only ever useful when I turned up with some paperwork at that delivery office one day to give to the DOM.

Boo! Hiss!

I also wasn't paid properly for the first four weeks.

Being a duty manager means that you get the lowest rate applicable for a Band 4, and adjustment is made from your normal wages to the new role. As a part timer in my usual role, this meant roughly a £200 increase as a manager.

Lovely jubbly.

Every week I'd be on the phone to the wages department who would promise to sort it out the following week and never did. On week five when I finally got the backdated pay and the issue was sorted I ended up with nearly a grand on top of my weekly wages. For a day or so that felt great until I then got a casual email saying that they'd just looked at my wages and it turned out I'd been overpaid by around three hundred quid and they would be

∞ CUTTING OFF ∞

taking that back at the rate of £50 per week for the next six weeks.

The full access required to use all the manager bits of the computer systems wasn't given to me until roughly a month before my tenure ended.

Within Royal Mail are a shadowy department called the Investigation Branch, or IB for short. They are the police of the company and their main role is to check no one is doing anything illegal in the course of their job.

One day at a large delivery office, nearly all the posties were out on delivery and I saw two people I didn't recognize, a man and a woman, stood near one of the frames. Their body language was weird and reminded me of how people acted in early silent movies (i.e. their movements were exaggerated). I walked over.

"Can I help you?"

The man smiles and reaches for his wallet and shows me an ID card. "Well done, Trojan Horse. We're from IB. Can I see your DOM please?"

We go to the DOM's office and the IB agent sucks air through his teeth and says "One of your posties let us in, a woman. Not good, think she's in trouble. Didn't ask for ID like Lance did".

The DOM stares at him for a moment and says "That's not fair, she knows your face. You've been in here before".

"Oh...yeah".

Duty managers also need to show willing if they want to

∞ CUTTING OFF ∞

be retained. The job is not permanent and for that reason I asked my home depot's DOM if he could put the word out that I was willing to work in neighbouring Sectors if needed.

The following week my own Sector was at capacity but happily a delivery office twenty five miles away needed a line manager for a week. Happy days. With a start time of 5.30am I was out of bed at 4 o'clock every morning, working until about 2.30pm. I vividly recall pulling over onto a parking bay on the bypass when driving home, reclining my seat and falling asleep for half an hour EVERY day.

The week after that I got what I thought was my big break. A Singleton unit needed a DOM for a day.

Whoopee!

Singletons have up to forty posties but are small enough to warrant only one manager, with a senior postie usually acting up on the DOM's day off. On the Monday afternoon I went over to meet the bloke I would be replacing. He was a Duty Manager like me and had been at the delivery office for about three weeks. He'd only been having Sundays off up to that point but had finally asked for his normal day off and they'd sent me to fill in for him. Perplexed as to why he'd worked six days a week without comment up to now he replied "Don't like to cause a fuss" which is presumably why they'd taken advantage of this. He also hadn't filed for the overtime for three days extra work. True to form this guy was still an acting manager long after I moved back to the ranks. He showed me what would be required of me when I got in the next day and then introduced me to the posties who were pouching off after coming back in. Turned out one was a guy I went to school with that I hadn't seen in 26 years. Now bald as an egg he'd gone straight into the Royal Mail from school and been there ever since. We had a quick chat and reminisced before I made my way out and home, ready for my first day as an acting DOM.

I got there at 6am to find a sheet of A4 with hand written notes about what the day would involve. One line said "Three walks to be absorbed". When the posties began to arrive I walked around introducing myself and mentioned the three routes on absorption, without realising the significance of that fact.

About 20 minutes later when I stepped out of the office again a grizzled looking postie approached me and said loudly "I've just got off the phone to the union. We agreed to absorb two Walks only, which means this is bullying!"

I look at him and extend my hand. "Sorry? Don't think we've been introduced. Name's Lance. Don't call me a bully when you don't even know my name".

He looks slightly uncomfortable but shakes my hand and in my peripheral vision I can see other posties unlatching themselves from their frames and starting to walk over to back him up. Realising I need to defuse this

∞ CUTTING OFF ∞

quickly I say brightly "That information was given to me on a sheet of paper that I've only just seen. If you agreed just two, I wasn't aware of it. Tell you what. We'll do two on absorption and the other on overtime. Acceptable?"

The guys walking up then stop where they are and the guy nods and says "That's fine", shakes my hand again and everyone drifts back to their frames.

Later on I had to find people to actually do the other Walk on overtime, which proved an uphill struggle. I asked the guy who'd challenged me and he laughed theatrically and then shouted "Hey everybody, you hear that? He just asked if I want any overtime?" His neighbours all chortle and he then says "I don't do overtime...EVER".

I got it covered eventually by about three different guys, including the one I went to school with and had to do about five streets myself.

Something that was commonplace for Duty managers was having to cover the posties' Cut Offs. By union agreement all overtime had to be offered to the OPGs first and then it fell to the Blue Meanies. For the first three weeks of my time as a Duty Manager I was out all except one day delivering mail. This in itself wasn't so bad as it was May, the weather was nice and it was pleasant to get out in from fresh air. The fly in the ointment was that I was in a suit in formal shoes that weren't designed for walking in and I'd come back all sweaty with sore feet.

Another thing unofficially expected of Duty managers

∞ CUTTING OFF ∞

was that they wouldn't ask for overtime. An hour here or there to show willing was something I was prepared to do but one day the posties went on strike and the managers from not only our sector but neighbouring ones as well had to jump into the breach.

The strike was at the one depot only AND was for only one hour but with eighty guys downing tools this meant we would lose eighty hours of work at the depot. The posties stood at the top of the driveway with the union rep and the duty managers took it in turns to stand nearby to watch that they didn't obstruct the traffic coming in or out.

To negate the lost time we had managers in from depots far and wide. Substantive managers weren't part of the same union as posties, meaning there was no conflict of interest. Duty managers however were but the union had agreed a long time ago that we wouldn't be expected to join strikes if wearing the blue waistcoats.

It became obvious just how serious the loss of manpower and time was, even for just 60 minutes, when by 8am I found we were on Dannycon 4.

In the Sector I worked in were four Dannys. All managers. Three were DOMs and one was a guy brought in when needed, to train people in the nuances of World Class Mail. To have all four under one roof for anything other than a meeting meant serious shit was going down.

We were all assigned a frame and told to throw up the Walk relevant to it. Like a Royal Mail version of the

∞ CUTTING OFF ∞

Avengers I remember seeing DOMs, ADOMs, line managers and even our DSM throwing up mail. Once the hour was up and the posties came back in, everyone then drifted back to their respective depots.

Surreal.

When I asked for the three hours overtime that this had caused me to work Peter the DOM tutted and glared at me, saying that he'd never had a Duty manager expect overtime before. I countered that anything up to an hour or so was on me but three was something I wanted paying for.

Due to the subtleties of the job I had asked repeatedly if I could attend the management training programme that Royal Mail ran a few times a year. After pestering the DSM's office for long enough I got a place on a course at the local university about 10 miles from my house. I was really pleased to have got this as it was kudos for future prospects and meant I'd be floundering less when sent to different delivery offices at short notice as I'd know the rules that governed the various management roles. The course lasted five days, Monday to Friday.

A week before I was due to go, I got an email from the DSM's secretary saying that I'd been moved from the course and placed on one in Sheffield instead, at the Royal Mail offices there. Perplexed as to why I spoke to her on the phone but she said she didn't know the reason but this had been invoked by someone called the Management

∞ CUTTING OFF ∞

Development Manager.

I later spoke to Peter who said that by happy coincidence, this guy was in an office two floors above us and I should nip upstairs and have a chat with him. Peter assured me that he'd had probably just made a mistake and would undoubtedly put me back on the course once I explained the situation to him.

I went up to the second floor and to a large, open plan office. At the far end was the man in question. He stood up smiling and appeared quite friendly up until he found out why I was there. His smile faded and he shook his head.

"Oh no, no. I've got my graduate managers booked in for that".

"But Sheffield's over a hundred miles away. I'll have to stay in a hotel, spend a fortune in cattery fees and it'll mess up my social life for a week".

He shakes his head like he's being chased by a mosquito and says again "They wouldn't want an outsider with them".

"How am I an outsider? We work for the same company, we're going to be doing the same job".

He pouts a bit and I notice that other people nearby are now listening in to this. He then adds "It would upset them".

"Excuse me? I'm a graduate myself. I've got a bachelor's degree in Law".

He looks like this is a violation of the Geneva

∞ CUTTING OFF ∞

Convention and shakes his head again. "They wouldn't want an outsider. It would upset them".

"You've kicked me off that course to make way for them. I was the first name down on the list. That's not fair".

He shakes his head again and with finality states "Unless there are welfare issues I don't want it to happen".

I look at him and realise I am going to have to simply suck this up. He's not going to budge and clearly believes he's the father to a flock of fledgling superheroes. How he imagines I'd "upset" them is beyond me. I walk off downstairs and tell Peter who looks shocked but goes "Oh well, talk to the DSM's office, see if they can get you a hotel".

A week later I attended the management training course over 100 miles away, with a fast track DSM sat next to me. I stayed in a nice hotel with nice meals and free use of a gym. I did however spend £85 on cattery fees I couldn't claim back and spent money on petrol, mobile data and phone calls that I didn't get back for three weeks.

While I was there I decided to try and sort out the issues I'd been having with computer access that was still trickling through the system. The department that handled it was based in the same building. On lunch one afternoon I went to see them and they were super helpful, saying they'd take a look into things and I should come back tomorrow.

∞ CUTTING OFF ∞

The following day I came back and while talking to the same guy, his supervisor came over.

"Hi mate, sorry. Can you stop this? I'm afraid you're not meant to be in here. We need to sort this type of thing out on the phone".

"But I'm physically here. I just thought it would be more efficient to come and discuss it with you face to face".

He looks embarrassed but adds "I agree but my manager just told me to ask you to leave, we could both get in trouble for letting you in here".

After I got back from Sheffield I also managed to bag a First Aid course and believed my CV would now be bursting with skills and training that would mean I'd be indispensable to the company.

Yeah, right.

∞ CUTTING OFF ∞

The End of the Line Manager

It turned out that by being away from the delivery offices for so long had been counter productive. A total of ten days (including days off) for training had meant that the rotas for who was placed where hadn't taken me into account. I tried to get something from the DSM's secretary and she pointed out that with it now being the back end of September, the holidays were over and less cover was needed but she'd see what she could do.

At the eleventh hour she got me a place in the original depot I'd worked in in May. Relieved, I got in on the Monday and things were relatively normal. On the Tuesday I found out that I was only needed for three days, and they would be cutting me loose to go back to being a postie on Thursday. As I'd been promised the entire week I went to see the DSM who was upstairs in his satellite office. After listening to what I had to say he reminded me that the role of a Duty Manager was something that meant I was only called upon when needed....and now I wasn't needed.

I countered that I'd been told I was working a full five days and that had been changed at less than two days notice. This would in turn affect my wages as I'd budgeted for what I'd been told I would receive.

He then goes off on a tangent about how difficult his job is as he has to work in managers everywhere and soon has to make spaces for the Graduate managers that are coming up. I realise this isn't going to go anywhere so I head back downstairs and just carry on with what needs to be done.

Two days later I was back as a postie and about halfway through the Walk my phone rang. It was the DSM's secretary asking if I'd be happy to go as a Duty Manager to a delivery office tomorrow morning. Like the sun breaking through the clouds this was awesome and I thanked her and said yes, indeed, I would love to.

Next day I was up at 5am, shoes buffed and shirt ironed and off to the delivery office. When I got there the DOM was surprised to see me.

"Don't think we need you Lance. We're at capacity today. Let me check".

Turned out I'd been double booked with another manager. Problem was that he was substantive, I was acting up, so he took precedence.

The DOM looks embarrassed but says "I'm sorry mate, you need to go back to your depot".

I sit in the chair opposite his desk, feeling deflated. After a pause I reply "I'm not a snob but do you have any idea just how soul destroying this is. I turn up in a suit, told I'm going to be a manager and now you're kicking me back to the streets, without notice and without pay?"

He looks uncomfortable and says "OK, you're right. This isn't on. You can stay today but you'll need to go back

∞ CUTTING OFF ∞

to your own office tomorrow".

For an hour I do my stuff until my mobile rings and it's my own DOM.

"Hello?"

"Hi Lance, sorry to do this to you. I know we said you could stay today but we are totally rammed here, too many guys off sick. We need you back here on delivery".

I can tell by the tone of his voice that he's being honest about this but I ask:

"Can you at least guarantee me manager's pay for today? I'm being cut loose with no notice I think it's the least Royal Mail can do".

"I agree. I'm not supposed to but I'll make sure you get it today for being messed about. Can you get back over here asap though".

I go to the DOM in his office and tell him what happened. He again looks embarrassed and shakes my hand.

"See you again maybe".

"Not unless I'm loaned out to you for a delivery. Days of unpaid overtime, up at half past cunt in the morning, management training, first aid training and now THIS?! I'm done".

He half smiles and says "Don't take it personally".

"I'm not. Royal Mail appear to fuck everyone over".

I dawdle as long as possible at home getting out of my suit and into uniform and then turn up at the delivery

∞ CUTTING OFF ∞

office.

Within an hour I'm out in the rain delivering mail, back to square one.

∞ CUTTING OFF ∞

Communal Misery

When I came in the following day, Peter, the DOM from the delivery office where I'd been shown the ropes as a Duty manager was now the ADOM and my line manager.

We had a quick chat to discuss what I'd been doing and what I'd be doing from now on and I then said:

"When I think about how badly I got treated as a manager I look at you and know it could have been a lot worse".

Peter had been boss of that delivery office for nearly a year in an acting capacity. He was a substantive level 4 and had not only held the fort but successfully run a very busy band 9 depot that was meant to be controlled by someone of the same pay grade as a DSM.

He'd always been calm and collected, never lost his temper and was quietly spoken throughout my time working for him. He'd had a higher graded manager working under him, had been responsible for seven junior managers including me and a whole shed load of posties.

I'd always respected him and especially admired his ability to remain calm no matter what was thrown his way.

One day I'd seen him in shorts as I was about to leave the delivery office and the next day I turned up in the same, it being a heatwave in the middle of June. After about five minutes he asked for a chat in his office and simply sat behind his desk smirking and looking me up

∞ CUTTING OFF ∞

and down.

"Errr...is this not appropriate?"

"No, you're a manager. Why are you in shorts?"

"You wore them yesterday, I assumed it was OK".

He chuckled and said "I changed into them to go home".

I am very embarrassed at this little faux pas and offer to change into the postie uniform I keep in the boot of my car in case I'm out on delivery (as I found out quickly that going postal in a suit wasn't pleasant).

He chuckled again and went "No it's OK, just wear trousers tomorrow".

For the rest of the shift you could occasionally hear someone bleating "But Lance is wearing shorts!" whenever a postie was rebuked for not wearing their hi-viz or not having Royal Mail issue footwear on.

Another time a 19 year old postie who had a reputation as a bit of a lad, came out of the line managers' office on the verge of tears saying "It's bullying and harassment, it's bullying and harassment".

Turned out he'd been criticised for something and had told the manager speaking to him to 'fuck off'.

Peter saw him emerge, asked the line manager what had happened and then said "Do you want me to suspend him?"

The line manager said "No, it's OK, can you just give him a written warning".

Calm and collected.

When the DSM decided to fill the DOM's vacancy full time, Peter applied for the role but didn't get it. To rub salt in it, the job went to a guy who applied from an outside company and resigned within three months of taking the role. Peter was now £500 a month worse off and his consolation prize after all that loyal service was to be the ADOM in a band 2.

As I say this he smiles and says "Put it this way. I've got a beautiful wife and four beautiful kids. I don't care".

As time moved on, Peter's calm demeanor began to slip. He became grumpy and bad tempered, sometimes raring up at me and other posties for relatively trivial things. After a couple of months he said to me, "I'm leaving. Back to delivery. I've had enough. Mortgage paid off, no need for this now".

Within a week of saying that he was back at the delivery office where he'd been a DOM...as a postie. Apparently on the first day the managers he'd once been the boss of had a meeting with him, wanting reassurance that he was OK with being an OPG in a depot he'd once controlled. He was never happier and apparently went back to smiling and being calm, content in his work.

Of the other managers I met who were acting up like I had, in the Duty capacity, a total of seven chose to return to the ranks, sick of the bullshit and how they were treated. One who was an Acting DOM of a Singleton unit told me

∞ CUTTING OFF ∞

that she was considering jacking in being a manager as she could make more money with two hours overtime per day, than she did as a temporary boss.

Sure enough, two weeks later she was back on the streets.

Graduate Managers

The Management Development Manager's fragile little chicks turned out to be a national phenomenon.

Along with most ideas that very senior management come up with, none of the rest of us really gave a shit unless it impacted on us. I met one of them a week before I relinquished the blue & orange waistcoat. Seemed pleasant enough. Male, 22, nervous as hell, called Jerome and still had spots.

When I was reassigned back to my home depot permanently, he was still there and it turned out that he was "making his bones" as a grade 4 manager and would then (provided he ticked all the boxes) be fast tracked up the ladder to a DSM or higher.

Chatting to him while bundling up one day and he said that there had been thousands of applicants for the role, with 15 of them getting selected after a fairly lengthy application & interview process. The company were spending a great deal of money on them with regard to training and they had to prove they had the "right stuff" within a short space of time.

Against the odds Jerome turned out to be a genuinely likeable chap. Whether they'd been told in their classroom not to throw their weight around was never revealed but he was always humble and never gave orders, simply asking us to do stuff or shadowing more experienced (and usually

∞ CUTTING OFF ∞

acting) managers to see how they dealt with things.

Within about three months he was moved on to pastures new and we got another one. This one was female, called Abigail, again 22 and looked about 18. She was a self confessed fan of One Direction but like her predecessor, not at all arrogant and proved popular with most of the staff (apart from those who had "managers are all cunts" hardwired into their DNA).

I got on all right with her and she wasn't shy on saying how she felt, albeit she never shouted or tried to invoke her rank, just made a concerted effort to get on with everyone.

One frigid January and I was in early throwing up a frame due to overtime. The internet had been off in the delivery office for a total of three weeks by this point and the new DOM (the fourth I'd seen since I'd been there) was having to travel to the neighbouring depot five miles away to check his emails. Whole thing was beyond ridiculous, especially as we were a Band 2 delivery office with over 100 staff.

Abigail was milling about near the parcels and she was making small talk with me. When she mentioned the internet not working I said "Last time the internet was working you were in high school".

She laughed but another female manager looked at one of the postwomen and went "Charming. He spoke to me like that I'd kick him in the balls".

I sighed, picked up my packets and went "I couldn't

give a fuck!" and walked off.

Behind me I could hear a shouted "WHAT?!!"

A few minutes later Abigail walked past my frame and I went "Did you think I was rude to you back there. If you think so, tell me and I'll apologise. I was only joking".

She smiled again and went "It's OK, I didn't mind. I knew you were joking. Don't worry".

I carried on throwing up, incident forgotten until the DOM appeared ten minutes later looking weary and said "Right, I'm really not in the mood for this. You're not in trouble BUT I've just had a complaint about how you speak to Abigail".

"Well I know it wasn't made by her because I just spoke to her and offered to apologise and she said she wasn't arsed".

"No, it wasn't her. I'm not telling you who it was but it was more than one person".

"In that case I know who they were then. Jesus Christ, if Abigail isn't bothered why are you even talking to me?"

He shakes his head and says "Like I said, I'm not in the mood. Just think about how you're perceived when you speak to people".

Another time I found out that while Abigail drove herself to work every day she couldn't drive Royal Mail vehicles as she hadn't done the requisite Change Over training. This situation was never rectified, right up to and beyond when she was shipped off to another Band 2

∞ CUTTING OFF ∞

delivery office as the DOM about a year later.

One day it was revealed that all the substantive managers were on holiday or on days off at the same time so Abigail was going to be the Acting DOM for two days. When she happily told me this I said "That isn't fair on the two Duty managers who are going to have to carry you. You haven't even done Change Over yet".

She looks a bit hurt and I added "You're good at your job but you're not ready yet. You know that. Have you even done a DODR yet? This is the DSM being a dick and putting you through too fast. You should at least have done Change Over by now".

"I don't have to do it, I'm a manager I'm not on deliveries".

"Yeah, right. You know as well as me that you lot are out most days doing our Cut Offs. You're invariably with one of the managers who can drive a van. posties need to know managers can be relied upon. Ever seen Master & Commander, the Russell Crowe movie?"

She shakes her head.

"Gun crews are commanded by Midshipmen. In the movie one gets wiped out by a cannon ball and the Captain takes his place until the battle's over. Point is, the Captain knows how to operate a cannon because he did that job. You can't drive posties to their start points or even drop mail off without someone with you. It's not good."

"Crap analogy but I get your point" she says before

∞ CUTTING OFF ∞

walking off.

Next day I came in at 10am and when she walked over I dropped to one knee and took my cap off.

"STOP BEING CHILDISH!!!"

One day I came in for work and she asked for a word in the managers' office. She looked embarrassed and was fidgeting a bit. As I sat down she went:

"I need to talk to you about thome letterth you brought back yethterday".

I wince and go "First of all can you lower your voice half an octave and stop lisping. You don't normally talk like that!"

She blushes and replies "I'm trying to be nithe".

Just then the DOM sticks his head in and proceeds to shout at me for the same reason, I shout back and after two minutes we agree that in future I'll try not to Cut Off and shake hands on the matter while Abigail seems relieved that she's no longer involved.

When she left the delivery office to go to pastures new, I gave her a Darth Vader mask with a voice changer in it as a going away present. When she looked confused at this I pointed out that when she was doing a Stage 3 sickness warning, talking to an irate customer, or suspending an OPG for suspected thievery, she should wear that mask as it would bless her with the required tone of voice to give people the willies, rather than remind them of Violet Elizabeth Bott from the TV show Just William.

∞ CUTTING OFF ∞

Email of Complaint to DOM

11th August 2015

FAO: DOM

Cc: Union Rep, Sub Union Rep

Dear DOM and all,

In light of the discussion I had yesterday, 10th August with line managers Grizelda, Ursula and Aubrey plus the DOM I have now decided to write this letter.

I do not feel this impromptu "meeting" was handled appropriately. In particular the way I was spoken to by Ursula (best comparison would be that she addressed me like she was talking to an errant schoolboy).

Also the fact that I was on more than one occasion asked questions by both her and Aubrey simultaneously and expected to keep up with both. The mitigation I cited at the time for bringing mail back on Saturday 8th August was almost completely ignored so here it is again in bullet points.

1. For the last 3 years I have always come in earlier on a Saturday than my start time from Monday to Friday (10am) at between 9 and 9.30am.

This is known to the managers and was suggested by the previous DOM when I started due to the earlier closing time of the delivery office on a Saturday.

∞ CUTTING OFF ∞

This allows for what I call "buffer time" where I can work over my paid 5 hours in the event of not being able to finish by my allotted time, and still get back before the office is locked up at 3pm. When I reminded Ursula on Friday 7th August that I would be in earlier the next morning she said words to the effect of "No, don't come in then come in at 10, we've got a lot of walks to prepare and we need time to get things ready." I stated that this would makes things tight if I needed to work over my time and she said words to the effect of "You always take your food relief at the end of your shift so if you come in at 10 you'll still have enough time."

2. I arrived at the office at 10am the next morning and was told by Aubrey that I was on Walk 21. I walked over to it and Ursula said to take it out. I pointed out that there were no parcels on the frame and she went over to the mini yorks and the packets hadn't been taken to the frame. She said words to the effect of "well spotted" and I took the york over and began to sort the packets when another OPG came over and said he was doing the Walk on overtime. Ursula then said he was doing it and I must be on Walk 20 instead. A few minutes later Aubrey then returned and said it was his mistake, apologised and told me I was on the Muckton 1 job.

Time spent on this = 10 mins (approx).

3. The packets hadn't been worked into the frame or the envelopes turned for the larger packets on the Muckton

∞ CUTTING OFF ∞

job. There were a lot of packets and when I flagged this up to Aubrey he said that the job "only takes two and a half hours" and it wouldn't take me long to sort out what hadn't been done. I then began to sort this out and asked Aubrey to print me off a map of where I was going as I hadn't done this job before, only having done the Muckton 3 and 4 Walks and even those I hadn't done for at least a year. I then pointed out that the Door To Doors hadn't been put in the frame and Aubrey said to leave them completely and not do them.

Time spent on this = 15 mins (approx)

4. When I finally got the Walk together I said I didn't know if I'd be able to complete in time, to Aubrey. He repeated that the Walk was "only two and a half hours" and very easy. I again countered that I hadn't done it before and had the commute plus a fair amount of Tracked parcels plus one Special Delivery that would take priority due to time restraints.

I stated the Walk might be 2.5 hours if I knew it, which I didn't but Aubrey repeated that it was easy. The map he gave me did not have the start point for the Walk marked on it.

I asked Aubrey where it was and he pointed to a part of the map but a short time later said words to the effect of "No, actually it's there" and pointed to a different part. I then took the Walk out but had to find van 19 which I'd been allocated, that wasn't in the loading bay or car park

∞ CUTTING OFF ∞

but parked up near Church Terrace on the road.

Time spent on this = 8 mins (approx).

5. Commuting to Muckton, Hillside (road)

Time spent on this = 17 mins (time obtained via Google maps)

6. I prioritised the Special Delivery and then began to work on the loops of mail that I had to deliver. Not knowing the area I had bundled up the mail corresponding to the roads on the frame. It turned out that there were two points where I had to return to the van and then drive to a different point.

The map I had been given by Aubrey did not list all the roads I was delivering to and I had to ask passers by for help in finding these roads. 5 or 6 of the packets I was given (some of which were Tracked) were very large and had to be taken separately from the mail afterwards as a special drop.

At 2.25pm I then returned to the delivery office and arrived upstairs at approximately 2.45pm. Aubrey was there with his daughter, and Harvard who locks up on a Saturday. As Aubrey had seen me walk in with a mini york with mail and packets visible in it, I did not feel it necessary to flag it up to him that I had brought mail back, having already told him this might happen before I went out. With only 10 minutes until the depot was locked until Monday morning I assumed the mail would not be taken out and delivered. This I now accept was a mistake on my

∞ CUTTING OFF ∞

part as I should have informed Aubrey formally and not assumed he had seen me and realised I had brought mail back.

Time spent commuting back from Muckton = 20 mins (approx)

7. The impromptu meeting yesterday was without advance notice and the points I've raised above were ignored. Some of the gems that Ursula came out with during her patronising rant at me for bringing mail back included that I shouldn't have done the Tracked parcels as a different run but taken them with the mail.

I pointed out that they were far too big to fit in the mail delivery pouches but she ignored me and repeated what she'd just said. She then said I shouldn't have done the Special Delivery first but put it in the mail and "done that loop first."

I countered that I didn't get the Special until after I'd bundled up when the mail was in boxes and pouches on a york, waiting to be taken downstairs. She then said I should have gone back and worked out what loop it belonged to and then put it in. I asked how I was meant to do that if I didn't know the Walk or what roads were on it. She replied I should have looked at the letter at the front of the bundles and found out that way. I countered that some bundles contain more than one road so this was not an effective method but she ignored me. She then said I "always bring mail back" and I countered that I don't and

∞ CUTTING OFF ∞

listed three Walks that it is acknowledged I can do effectively without cutting off. Ursula then began to interpret everything I said literally and replied with words to the effect of, "So out of 100 plus walks there's three that you can do in this office then?" Aubrey then mentioned the possibility of re training and Ursula said words to the effect of "Ooh yes, maybe we should retrain you."

I then walked out and approached the DOM who had been in the meeting but had left just before the subject of retraining came up. I was then told by the DOM and Aubrey that the delivery office kept failing and this was in part due to me bringing mail back "all the time."

I have calculated from the times I listed above, that the time wasted on Saturday through no fault of mine, plus the commutes to Muckton and back, came to one hour and ten minutes approximately. Adding meal relief time of 30 minutes this means that one hour and forty minutes were already gone from my shift before I started. Ursula and Aubrey both said that half an hour could be added to the shift to allow for the packets, bringing the estimated two and a half hours that they think the shift should take, up to three hours. As I had three hours twenty minutes of active time left to deliver mail, I think you can know see that our figures more or less match.

To sum up. I didn't know the Walk having never done it before. I had to be back by 3pm or the delivery office would have been locked and I would have had no way to get in.

∞ CUTTING OFF ∞

I was specifically told by a manager (Ursula) to not turn up until 10am on Saturday so things would be ready for me which they weren't. I also didn't have an accurate map.

Also, in light of how Ursula spoke to me yesterday I am no longer prepared to have any further discussions with her unless someone of my choice is also present at the time.

Yours,

Lance Manley

Arse Over Tit

In 2001 while kickboxing I snapped the anterior crusciate ligament in my left knee. I got it seen to, was booked in for an operation in 2004 and at the last minute the surgeon called off the op, saying that the leg was healthy. Having no medical knowledge I assumed that this meant the knee had healed by itself. What it actually meant was that the heavy cycling I was doing on a daily basis in central London had strengthened the leg enough to compensate.

As I got older the leg got more painful in cold weather and as a postie I'd sometimes have to wear a knee support. By 2014, when it became clear that this wasn't something that was simply going to go away on it's own I again went to a doctor who referred me to the knee clinic of the local hospital and I got on the waiting list for keyhole surgery to repair the ACL.

Despite what many people say about the NHS in the UK, the service I got was top notch. My wait couldn't be more than a maximum of 12 weeks and I could even postpone by up to 6 weeks if I was unavailable. Anything over that though and you had to reapply from scratch.

I was on the waiting list when, by an unhappy coincidence, I happened to have what it politely described as an Industrial Accident, 10 days before the scheduled operation.

The elevators at my home depot were two big,

∞ CUTTING OFF ∞

cumbersome old monsters. Both broke down at least once a month and I knew various people who'd ended up trapped in them for an hour or so until ROMEC swooped in to extract them.

The doors opened up & down, not side to side and you got in one end at the bottom and out the other end at the top. The doors had to be closed manually once you got out, or the lift couldn't be summoned from the other level. Anyone pushing the 'Call' button would hear the sound of a bell which was meant to a). Tell them the door was open and b). Tell whoever was at the other end to close the doors. This sometimes led to people irately playing tunes on the thing and swearing as they tried to attract attention before throwing in the towel and actually walking down to shut the doors themselves.

The bottom door on one elevator would sometimes bounce back up about four inches after opening. This issue was occasionally addressed by ROMEC but it kept coming back.

At the end of one shift I had a york of parcels to bring back and as the lift arrived I went to pull the trolley in behind me. As I stepped in, I caught my left foot on the protruding door and went down hard on the floor, luckily managing to twist and slam my forearm on the deck as a break fall. My knee twisted hard and hurt like hell. As I lay there swearing a guy who was on the loading dock came over and his initial amusement quickly evaporated when

∞ CUTTING OFF ∞

he saw I was in pain.

"You OK?"

"Nope, that fucking door again. Stupid cunts have never fixed it".

I got up and closed the doors, then rode the elevator up to the first floor and hobbled into the managers' office. All of them were still there along with the DOM. One put an ice pack out the First Aid kit on my leg while another went to check on the elevator. After asking if I was OK I then got the predictable question:

"Are you wearing appropriate footwear?"

I raise my uninjured leg off the floor to show that yes, I am indeed wearing Royal Mail issue trainers.

They then took photos of my knee, my grazed elbow where I'd landed on the floor, my feet to prove I had the correct footwear on...and then got me to stand in the lift to 're-enact' the moment.

I limped home and at exactly 8am the next day rang my doctor's surgery for a standby appointment. They always hold spaces on the actual day for people who need urgent but non life threatening medical help. After the third try I got through and there was an appointment at 9.10 that morning.

As I was about to set off the DOM rang me.

"Can you stop by the delivery office today please?" he asks. "We need to do the paperwork for yesterday".

I pointed out that the surgery was just down the road

from the delivery office so no problem, I'd nip in afterwards.

The doctor was concerned, probing and prodding my sore knee. When he found out my operation was in just over a week he wrote me a sick note stressing that I needed strict rest until my operation and was absolutely not to go to work. He mentioned that strain had been placed on the existing injury and if this was made worse then I could end up with my operation postponed or cancelled if they couldn't perform surgery due to the swelling. He also gave me a prescription for some kickass painkillers.

I then made my way to the delivery office where the DOM and a female line manager read my sick note and then took me into the ADOM's office and proceeded to ask me some questions.

It went like this:

"So can you tell us what happened?"

I tell them what happened.

"But don't you look where you're going. Surely you could see that the door was sticking up".

(Pause) "Ah, I see. Right! Err...I'm not a penguin, I don't tend to look straight down when I walk. I, like most human beings over the age of 2, tend to look in front of me for obstacles".

"Were you wearing appropriate footwear?"

"We've already established that I was, you have photos".

∞ CUTTING OFF ∞

"How did you get here today?"

"I drove".

"So you can drive then? Surely you could come to work in that case?"

"Err no...I drove because it's pissing down with rain and I considered it better to hobble to the car and then drive to the doctor's than get piss wet through and walk the whole way. It's a five minute drive or a twenty minute walk".

"But you drove here as well".

"As a favour to you, remember?"

"Could you not come in and do light duties? We could find you something to do that wouldn't put stress on your leg".

"Again no, as I have an operation coming up and my GP has specifically said I should rest completely".

This went on for about half an hour, with them asking the same questions at least twice. I was then told that the Occupational Health department would be ringing me either today or tomorrow and their professional opinion took precedence over my own doctor's. If I was to ignore them then I would potentially be in breach of regulations and could be fired.

Nice.

They then wrap things up and their demeanors change back to being friendly and chatty. I note the change in attitude and the DOM says brightly, "Oh don't take it

∞ CUTTING OFF ∞

personally".

I then make my way home and after less than an hour the phone rings. It's Occ Health and a cheerful sounding woman then talks me through what she's about to discuss. We go through the situation, what my doctor said and the fact I have an operation schedule soon. After about ten minutes she then says:

"In my opinion, one hour a day on very light duties would do you good. I'll tell them to give you something that won't put strain on the leg. It will do you good to be out of the house for a while each day".

I didn't like this but accepted it, after having been warned that her opinion carried more weight than that of my own doctor.

It was a while before I found out that she should at the VERY least have spoken directly to my GP before overruling his decision and that she had no right to form a professional opinion just from chatting to me on the phone for a few minutes.

Next day I limped down to the delivery office at 12pm and was expecting to be placed on a chair, throwing Door to Doors into frames.

But no.

Being short staffed they had decided to put me in the Packet Office covering the break of the woman who normally worked there.

I pointed out that I was in intense pain, on drugs and

∞ CUTTING OFF ∞

was, to put it mildly, a bit grumpy. The line manager insisted I'd be fine and that I wasn't to lift any heavy packets.

I turned up and relieved the woman on duty, who went off to the staff room for her sandwiches.

This wasn't appropriate, not least of all as I was still required to move about to fetch things but I thought I could work around it.

This went on for a few days and then, three days before my scheduled operation, I got a phone call from the hospital to say that it had been postponed by a week.

I was beyond angry about this but there was nothing that could be done. I informed the DOM I'd still be able to attend my Very Restricted duties and limped in each day, my leg hurting badly and then the inevitable happened.

A woman came in with a surcharge card. This meant the item had either not had enough postage paid when it was mailed, or had been grabbed by customs at the international border. I punched up the details on the computer and went and found her item.

"That's £15.20 please".

"I've already paid it," she snaps.

Stapled to the surcharge card is a folded piece of paper, the print out of her receipt to prove she paid online.

"Oh, I'm sorry I didn't see that".

She glares at me through the hatch and then says, "You were supposed to deliver that yesterday!"

∞ CUTTING OFF ∞

Her tone is getting right on my tits so I answer back "I wasn't supposed to do anything, I'm on restricted duties due to being injured".

"I didn't mean you, I meant the company. You're very rude".

"No I'm not".

The man in the queue behind her then pipes up.

"Yes, you are. That was rude".

The woman then waggles her finger at me and says, "Now listen to me young man!"

"I'm 45 next birthday. Don't call me 'young man', old lady!"

"Right! I'd like to speak to a manager please!"

"Fine" I reach for my phone and begin calling Carol, one of the line managers.

As I'm doing so the woman turns to the guy behind her and says "They're usually so lovely in here. I don't know where they found him!"

I drop the window hatch with a clang and they both jump and then she goes "Hah!"

As Carol's phone starts ringing I say through the glass "I'm trying to remain professional here. You gobbing off about me right to my face really isn't helping with that".

"Huh! You call that professional?"

The phone is answered; I tell Carol the situation, and then ask if she can come down.

She arrives after a couple of minutes and I say, "Can

∞ CUTTING OFF ∞

you do this where I can't hear you?"

Carol nods and moves to go outside with the offended woman and her witness. The guy looks at me and says, "Not too late to say sorry mate".

"Not gonna happen. And don't forget your credit card". I point to the card he'd left on the counter when he paid for his item. He looks surprised but picks it up then thanks me.

For the next half an hour Carol sat with this woman on the wall outside the packet office. I later found out that she got her a cup of tea, was seen with her arm around her and apparently Carol also got a witness statement off the bloke.

While Old Ladygate was happening, posties were returning to the office to drop off their packets and at least two came in chuckling after seeing what was going on. The guy who'd been there when I fell over the elevator door was laughing as he said "I knew it was you as soon as I heard her say 'I've never been spoken to like that in my life'. Hurr! Hurr! She's crying out there. Heard her say she's only 56 and didn't like being called an old lady".

Suspension

In the aftermath of the anarchic chaos that was that argument, I headed upstairs and loitered in the line manager's office waiting to give "my side of the story." Apparently being called an "old lady" by a postman was just too much for the woman.

I imagined the same manager would be dealing with the statement but instead, after about 15 minutes, another one detaches himself from his PC and grabs a notepad and paper.

"Come on then, let's get this over with."

"I thought Carol would be dealing with this, don't you want some semblance of continuity?"

"She's busy, we need to do this now, come on."

I stand where I am as he heads towards the door and then stutters to a halt when he realises I'm not following him.

"I'm not talking to you on my own, as the union are busy I'll get someone else."

He sighs and goes "Go on then" and I head off onto the shop floor. I had asked both the union rep and the sub rep to sit in with me and both were busy. Management can't force posties to see them in private and you are at the very least entitled to have a colleague or "friend" with you to sit in. This, in theory, means they can't lie about what they said or use tactics such as manipulation or coercion. I had sat with managers before without anyone else there, where silly behaviour had resulted so this time I was determined to have a witness.

Walking up the floor I knew my options were limited as most guys would now be out on delivery. However, to my immense joy I find Red Kev is still here, finalising his Walk and bundling up. Red Kev is semi legendary in the depot. He detests managers and when I got the acting manager's role I had bumped into him at a party for a local pub owner we both knew, and went over to say hi. The following conversation happened.

Me: "Alright mate?"

Red Kev: (Sucking air through his teeth) "Really don't want to talk to you, you're a manager."

Me: (I'm a bit drunk so I'm not sure if he's merely taking the piss): "What you object to me wanting a bit more money?"

Red Kev: (Shaking his head) "Nothing against you personally but I really don't want to talk to you, you're a manager."

Me: "My rank is OPG, you object to me wanting a bit more money?"

One of his mates then pipes up "Come on lads, not here, let's not be childish."

Me: "I agree."

His mate looks at me and says flatly "Well, fuck off then."

∞ CUTTING OFF ∞

I realise this isn't a joke and I'm not welcome so say "We're going to the pub soon, tell you what, We can ignore each other in there too." I then walk off feeling a bit embarrassed but forgot about it pretty quickly. Me and Kev ignored each other after that until about three months later in the pub when he walked up to me and tapped me on the arm.

"Sorry about what happened, I was out of order, I owe you an apology.

I'm quite surprised at this but extend my hand. "Thanks, you were being a miserable git but I appreciate you saying sorry, no hard feelings."

He shakes my hand, pauses then goes "I stand by everything I said but I was out of order".

I look at him puzzled "You apologising or not?"

"Yeah, but I stand by what I said."

After that we would say hello at the depot and eventually began chatting again and the incident was never brought up. Now, ironically, Red Kev is my salvation for the High school charade I'm about to go through.

"Alright Kev?

He turns to face me and smiles. "Yeah, not bad you?"

"Err...I'm about to get told off. Union are busy, you mind sitting in with me?"

His face lights up and he says "No problem", putting down a handful of letters without even pausing. We go back to the line managers' office and the world-weary

∞ CUTTING OFF ∞

manager then walks with us to the vacant DOM's office. He sits in the DOM's Blofeld chair while me and Kev sit the other side. As me and Kev are both in shorts this feels more and more like getting a bollocking from the Headmaster.

The manger takes the top off his biro and turns to a fresh page in his A4 notepad. "Right we need to have a fact finding meeting about you upsetting that woman earlier."

My temper frays immediately and I snap "You need to moderate your terminology. This is "fact finding" and that means you don't make sweeping statements that imply you already think I'm guilty."

He sighs again and then says "OK, we need to talk about how she says that you upset her."

"That's better" I turn to Kev. "What do you think?"

He shrugs, glances at the manager then says "I wouldn't say anything without the union present."

The manger then tries a tactic I'd anticipated and goes "You don't need the union Lance, this is merely fact finding."

I look at Kev again who simply repeats "I wouldn't say anything without the union present."

I know this will simply drag on if I don't deal with it now but there's no sodding way I'm going into this without proper advice. I decide on a middle ground and take my mobile phone out. "I tell you what, I'll call the Area rep and see what he says. I he OKs it then I'll stay."

∞ CUTTING OFF ∞

The manager shrugs again, clearly beyond boredom with the whole thing and I put the phone on speaker. After three rings it's answered. After introductions I state the situation and on speaker the rep says "No, it's OK, this isn't a judgment, it's merely fact finding. You got someone there with you?

"Yeah, Red Kev."

He chuckles at this and replies "No problem, just state your side of it, if it goes any further then ask for one of us to sit in with you."

I hang up and we begin. The manager writes down what I say and at the end after asking if I have anything else to add he starts to read it to us.

"What are you doing?"

"I need to read it to you Lance so you know it's accurate."

"Jesus! I'm not into audio books and I'm not 6 years old. Just let me read it, if I disagree with what you've written I'll tell you."

He slides the paper over to me and I read it, pointing out a couple of things he's not written down correctly, which he amends. Kev then reads it and we both sign it. As we're doing this the DOM sticks his head in and says "Lance can I see you in the ADOM's office when you're finished?"

We conclude it, I get a photocopy of what the manager wrote down and I shake Kev's hand then make my way to

∞ CUTTING OFF ∞

the ADOM's office. The DOM is looking pissed off and as I walk in he hands me three sheet of A4, still warm from the printer.

"I'm suspending you." he says without preamble.

My temper rises. Throughout all the pain I'd been in, the fucking lack of sleep and the painkillers that were all because of an accident that was Royal Mail's fault and the idiots put me in a situation where I was required to be nice to people. And this was AFTER they got Occ Health to overrule my own doctor's opinion. I glare at him as I look quickly at the forms. They cite the criteria for what is known as Precautionary Suspension and on page three it states that I am being suspended for alleged "inappropriate" and also "threatening" behaviour. I look up.

"You really are a pratt aren't you?"

He looked gobsmacked but then says "Don't speak to me like that, you're in enough trouble as...."

"You KNEW how much fucking pain I was in. You knew I was grumpy as hell and I haven't been sleeping. I sodding told you that. And you put me in a customer-facing environment. What did you think was going to happen?"

"You can't speak to people like that. You upset that woman. I've told you before about the way you talk to people."

"I'm in intense pain. My doctor signed me off but you shit me up with your horror stories about what would

∞ CUTTING OFF ∞

happen if I ignored Occ Health's opinions. And while we're on the bastard subject, since when can a doctor's decision be overruled just by talking to the patient for ten minutes?"

He looks embarrassed and then says "It's Precautionary, you'll be on full pay. It's not saying you're guilty."

"Doesn't sound like it. Christ! Would you have put a guy in a wheelchair on lifeguard duty? People in pain do not make good conversationalists. That woman was rude to me, all I did was retaliate. You've known me a while and you know I'm polite unless people cross the line. Calling someone 'old lady' is hardly bad news is it?"

"What do you think I should do then?"

"How about reinvoking my original sick note until the operation, or even showing some sodding objectivity?"

I glance at the forms again and see the word "threatening."

"How am I supposed to have been threatening her? I was behind three inches of bulletproof glass! I'm not Hannibal Lecter."

"This is done now, you need to leave the premises. I'll get someone to escort you out."

"Not until you tell someone of my choice you've done this." I walk out the office and he follows me up to Red Kev's frame. I turn to the DOM and say "So...tell Kev what you just told me."

∞ CUTTING OFF ∞

He clears his throat and says "Kevin, I'm now precautionary suspending Lance for alleged threatening and inappropriate behaviour." Kev snorts and then carries on bundling his Walk. The DOM turns to me "Happy now?"

"Ecstatic."

I walk over to the line managers' office and all three are in there. Everyone looks embarrassed. The bloke who led the meeting is nearest to me and I extend my hand "No hard feelings, you were just doing your job." He smiles and shakes my hand and then I turn to Carol. "Gizza hug, won't see you for ages." She does and then the DOM reminds me I need to leave. I unclip my ID badge and lay it on the table. "Want my gun as well? If I'd known this was going to happen I'd have brought a water pistol."

"Wouldn't trust you with a gun" he says, half laughing.

"I ain't shaking your hand" I glare at him and he looks a bit hurt but then moves off.

The remaining manager then gets up.

"Come on Lance, I'll escort you out."

She takes me down the stairs and to the security door. I bend forward slightly as I stand in the doorway. "Want to boot me up the arse as I go?"

She smiles and says "Don't be silly. You going to be alright getting home?"

"I'll be OK. See you around."

∞ CUTTING OFF ∞

She smiles and shuts the door after me and I limp home.

Aftermath

The following week I had my operation as planned. The whole thing was done in about 14 hours and I got a taxi back home before hobbling up to my flat on a pair of crutches that I'd been given a crash course in how to use by two nurses.

The pain was fucking horrible for about two weeks and felt like a mixture of toothache and sunburn in my knee. I was on three separate types of painkillers plus for 10 days I had to inject my own belly with an anti-coagulant to keep my blood from clotting.

Happy times.

About a week after my suspension a letter arrived from the DOM asking me to come in for a disciplinary meeting with regard to the incident in the packet office.

I consulted the Area union rep, who I'd never spoken to before and he advised me to refuse as I was now too sick to come in due to my convalescence. The delicious thing was that they kept writing to me and as they were sending the letters Special Delivery, if I wasn't in they'd leave a card to say to come and collect it. However I was banned from the premises due to my suspension so could legitimately NOT collect the letter as I wasn't allowed to enter the premises to do so.

After three failed attempts to get me to come in for a meeting the Area union rep spoke to me again on the phone and was laughing as he said:

"They hate you right now. Their problem is that you are suspended but also sick but you're too sick to come in and be unsuspended. Sick leave only lasts 6 to 12 months but a precautionary suspension on full pay can last indefinitely".

After two weeks I got a call from the DOM, I was expecting this to be another attempt at chiding me over my suspension but it turned out he was just checking I was OK.

Finally after six weeks he rang me to revoke my precautionary suspension and formally place me on sick leave.

"You're not suspended any more. It's still a disciplinary issue, we'll need to have a meeting about it when you get back but it's no longer sackable".

"It wasn't anyway. You should have heard the union laughing when I told them why you'd suspended me".

I continued to have phone calls with Occ Health at Royal Mail plus visits to specialists of their choice to evaluate my knee. As time moved on I was getting fatter, laying in the sofa binge watching TV shows like Sons of Anarchy and Breaking Bad.

It was very boring.

I'd also consulted the union about suing Royal Mail for my elevator injury and this was ongoing with both the legal firm representing me and my employers finding people to evaluate my condition. Surprisingly, Royal Mail admitted liability for the accident almost immediately but it still took just under a year for my compensation to be agreed. The main factor affecting any decision was that the operation had effectively healed any damage done by the injury, so they were paying for the fact they'd caused it and not any disability because of it.

After six months you are meant to drop down to half pay if on long-term sickness but as the accident had been their fault, the union argued I was entitled to another six months. After a total of seven months on the sick, a doctor phoned me from Occupational Health and said that in his opinion I would not be fit for duty within another year.

The magic words.

I rang the union rep who said that it was odds on I'd get an invite to attend a meeting for voluntary medical retirement within 12 hours.

Ten hours later a Special Delivery letter was in my mail box (the postie had apparently been under the instruction to leave it and sign the PDA himself if I wasn't in) inviting me to attend a meeting with the DOM.

I got the union rep to come with me and the DOM took us into his office, handed us three sheets of A4 paper and asked us if we'd be so kind as to go into another room to discuss what they said.

Once we moved next door, it was as I'd guessed. Voluntary retirement due to ill health. One year's pay as severance. Nine weeks pay in lieu. Shares released early

∞ CUTTING OFF ∞

and whatever pension I've earned in just over four years. Also officially marked as a Good Leaver. The union rep advises me to take it and we go back. The DOM smiles and offers me a cup of tea and as I'm waiting he goes to get the final forms for me to sign (printer is in an office 200 yards away). He comes back and I chat about a few things. I also say that the previous DSM (his former boss) should be retroactively aborted; not to put people in the Packet Office who are on painkillers; and that I have nothing against him personally but maybe he should get a less stressful job, like governor of a category A prison.

He says, standing up, "So no hard feelings, to be honest I'm going to miss the banter. Putting you in the packet office probably wasn't one of our better plans".

"I got you a going away present" I say and hand him a mug with a troll-esque face on the side as a parting gift. The words 'You in the morning' are on the tag. He smiles again and I knock back the remnants of the cup of tea.

"I'll drop my uniform and other crap in tomorrow if you want, I only live round the corner and it saves you sending some poor sod to pick it up."

"That's fine, thank you. I'll also need you to sign the Official Secrets Act".

We say our goodbyes and I have a few final, private words with the union rep then do a quick visit to the shop floor to say farewell to the few people still in the building.

∞ CUTTING OFF ∞

Glossary

'A' Job- A Walk created from Walks that are deemed too heavy to handle. Bits will be cut off three or four jobs until a new one emerges. These are bastards as the Walk is usually spread out over non-adjoining areas. There were three at my delivery office called Frankenstein, The Beast, and The Cunt.

Absorption- Putting bits of unassigned Walks into other people's jobs so that they get delivered. A really shitty way of making people do overtime without paying them for it.

ADOM- Assistant Delivery Office Manager. Only found in the bigger depots.

Appropriate Footwear- Royal Mail issued trainers or boots. Used as a loophole to avoid paying compensation to people who get injured at work. I.e. if they were wearing their own shoes without authorization from management, they'll get fuck all in any injury claim, regardless of why it was caused.

Banding- How a delivery office is ranked. Range from 4 (Singleton) up to 1 (Big) and then a 9 (Enormous). Never said it was easy to understand.

∞ CUTTING OFF ∞

Blue Meanies- Managers. So called because they wear blue and orange hi viz waistcoats with "Manager" emblazoned on the back.

Bundling Up- Getting ready to go out on delivery by putting the mail in bundles.

Cage- Where Special Deliveries, van keys, PDAs and anything requiring a signature are kept. Only authorized persons are allowed to enter unaccompanied.

Change Over- Being tested again (provided you have a full, UK driving licence) to prove you can be trusted to drive a Royal Mail vehicle.

Cutting Off- Leaving some of your Walk on the frame due to time issues. The BIGGEST source of arguments between posties and managers, mainly as the latter have to do it if they can't find anyone else to.

CWU- Communication Workers union.

Dannycon 4- There were four managers all named Danny in the sector I worked in. If all were in one depot at the same time for anything other than a meeting, you knew things were bad.

∞ CUTTING OFF ∞

Dark Side- As in, "he's gone to the dark side" meaning someone has become a manager.

Dead Walk- Nothing to do with zombies. When your Walk consists of walking without delivering, due to either having to commute to a new starting point or doubling back after having finished a Loop.

DODR/ Delivery Office Daily Report- A report from every delivery office to the DSM's secretary. All to give a clearer picture of how the Sector is performing. Have to be done at 10am and 1pm with the latter being of greater importance. Details include sickness absence, mail volume, cut offs and how many yorks are in the building.

Dock- Area where loading/ unloading occurs and vans are parked. Between 9 and 10am, in bigger depots, they resemble the opening scene of Saving Private Ryan.

Docket- Card left at a house if you weren't in when the postie arrived to deliver your parcel/ signature mail. Despite what the public may think, posties take no joy in leaving these things as it means more work when they have to take the parcel back.

DOM- Delivery Office Manager. The boss at the depot.

∞ CUTTING OFF ∞

Door To Doors- That free shit you get that most people just bin. Invariably involve Specsavers, Domino's Pizza and Uber. Take ages to put in the frame but have to be done.

Downstreaming- Some firms that do their own deliveries, still use Royal Mail for some of it. E.g. Letters sent from Scotland to Birmingham via the private company are then "downstreamed" to RM for the final part of the delivery when it is necessary to break the shipment up into individual addresses.

DSM- Delivery Sector Manager. A DOM's boss.

Duty Manager- A postie (or other member of Royal Mail staff) who is "acting up" in the role of a manager temporarily. One surefire way to lose most of your friends at work.

Flats- Magazines or newspapers that are put in other bits during Sorting as they're too big to go in the normal bits.

Floater- postie without a designated Walk who comes in and takes out whatever's left in the delivery office. Starts later than everyone except other Floaters and is usually part time.

Frame- The main apparatus used to prepare a Walk.

∞ CUTTING OFF ∞

Ghost Overtime- Working overtime within your normal hours. E.g. You are so good at your job you finish a 4 hour shift in 2 and then do 2 hour's extra work meaning you get paid for 6 hours. Long since abolished due to attempts to be frugal with the budgets.

Good Leaver- Someone who leaves employment with Royal Mail on good terms with the company (meaning they can get a positive reference or even come back if both sides wish it).

Graduate managers- The Hunger Games meets Big Brother. Usually in their early 20s, with bachelor degrees of at least upper 2nd class honours. Shoehorned into delivery offices on fast track to DSM roles. One at my home depot was female, 22, liked One Direction and looked like Pippy Longstocking.

Gun- See PDA.

HCT- High Capacity Trolley, Big red thing on wheels with two compartments to hold mail, packets, your waterproof clothes and lunch. Still isn't vast enough to hold most modern deliveries.

Home Depot- The one you are normally based at.

∞ CUTTING OFF ∞

Huddle- Taking a group of posties and telling them something. Used by managers to impart information so that not everyone has to down tools and stop working at the same time.

IB- Investigation Branch. The internal police of Royal Mail. Usually brought in if someone is accused of stealing but will occasionally turn up for a Trojan Horse. Have certain powers of entry to search private property.

Industrial Accident- Danger originating from technological or industrial accidents, dangerous procedures, infrastructure failures or certain human activities, which may cause the loss of life or injury, property damage, social and economic disruption or environmental degradation. Or so Google says.

Level 4- Lowest rank of Manager. Most Singleton depots have these as the DOM.

Line of Sight- Being able to see something. This basically means you can't be suspended, sacked or told off if you were still able to see your van or trolley and someone stole from it (e.g. when walking up a driveway).

Loop- A circuit of delivery (usually one bag) on a Walk.

∞ CUTTING OFF ∞

Medical Retirement- You are dismissed from the company due to illness, however it's not your fault and you will 99% of the time be marked as a Good Leaver if this happens.

OPG- Operational Postal Grade. A Postman or Postwoman.

Packet Office- Where mail and packets are kept if you weren't in when the postie tried to deliver your item(s). Also covers surcharged items and stuff needing payment for customs tax. I once had to charge an old man £1.01 for his wife's birthday card that had been 1p short on the postage. Not a proud moment.

Packet Run- Delivering only parcels.

PDA- Postal Digital Assistant. Handheld device used to scan packets and anything needing either tracking or a signature. Mine rang once and it was some guy trying to sell car insurance. Turns out they contain a SIM card. Who knew?

Pimps- Another word for managers.

Pouch Off- What you do when you get back to the depot. Involves putting any packets into the Packet Office and handing in your van keys, gun, and log book. Also a good idea to check the pockets of your delivery bag for anything

∞ CUTTING OFF ∞

you might have forgotten because if management find a Special in there once you've gone, you are well and truly fucked.

Precautionary Suspension- If you are accused of something naughty and your presence at work may compromise an investigation into the allegation, you are suspended on full pay until it is resolved.

Prepping- See throwing up.

Redirections- When people move house they sometimes pay Royal Mail to forward their mail to their new address. This consists of the postie putting stickers with the new info over the old. Simple.

Repicks- Every so often the Walks are 'up for grabs' and posties choose which ones they want to do. The most senior OPGs get first, second and third dibs which, as some have been there 30 or 40 years, means new guys get the leftovers.

Restricted- Being at work but on lighter or confined duties due to recent or ongoing illness.

ROMEC- The SWAT team of getting things fixed. Outsource company of handymen and women.

171

∞ CUTTING OFF ∞

Rough Sack- Sack like you'd put spuds in. Used to hold mail or parcels temporarily as they are moved from A to B.

Safe Drop- Somewhere deemed OK by management for mail to be left so a postie can collect it later on his or her Walk. Range from the front porches of houses to the bit behind the freezer in the local corner shop.

Sector- A group of delivery offices.

Sick, On The- Being off due to illness.

Signed For- Mail requiring a signature. Special Delivery's younger brother.

Singleton- A Delivery Office with only one manager.

Sorting- Getting mail out of boxes, yorks, and bags and into the cubbyholes corresponding to various Walks.

Special Delivery- Mail guaranteed for ATTEMPTED delivery by either 9am or 1pm the next working day. Some of the public don't seem to see the connection between "not being in" and having to come and collect it from the depot.

Sting- Operation conducted by both IB and managers to

∞ CUTTING OFF ∞

catch people accused of stealing. Happened twice at the delivery office I worked in. Both times it involved planting money/ valuables in letters on a postie's frame and then waiting to see if they pinched them.

Sub Rep- A Union rep is understudied by a sub rep. Similar principle as an Appointed First Aider.

Team Leader- In larger depots this will be the person responsible for giving training to posties and bringing those who weren't at the weekly meetings up to speed. Range from genuinely nice guys who enjoy helping people, to arrogant twats who like having a bit of authority.

Throwing up- Putting the mail in the frame.

Tracked- Mail or packets that have to be delivered by the end of the working day, (or delivery attempted). A poor man's version of Special Delivery.

Trojan Horse- Attempts by members of IB to gain access to a delivery office without showing ID. Anyone letting them in without challenging will later be in deep shit.

Walk- A postie's route to deliver mail.

Wilful Delay- Deliberately not delivering mail when you

∞ CUTTING OFF ∞

knew you had to. Suspendable or even sackable. Gets unpleasant when Management try to invoke this because you accidentally left something in your bag the day before, even though everyone knows it was a just a mistake.

Work Time Learning- Weekly meeting where posties are brought up to speed on changes in company policy, any new regulations or working methods, and sometimes shown a patronising video with crap actors about how awesome it is to work for Royal Mail.

York- Big, upright trolley thing used to hold parcels and/ or boxes. Smaller versions are used to hold packets for an individual Walk.

∞ CUTTING OFF ∞

About the Author

Lance Manley is from England and worked as a police officer from 2004 to 2008, and was on duty with the City of London Police on July 7th 2005 in the aftermath of the terrorist attacks. This job was the subject of his first book *Stab Proof Scarecrows*.

In 2010 Lance took up the Israeli self defence system of Krav Maga and holds the grade of Practitioner level 5 in the discipline. Krav was the subject of his 2016 book *Walk in Pieces* (a pun on the unofficial motto of Krav Maga, *"So that one may walk in peace"*).

In 2011 Lance taught English in Tampico, Mexico which led to a book entitled *The Cockroach Effect: Life in the Tampico Drug Wars*, co-written with Diana Aquino, the mother of one of Lance's students.

Lance is also the author of two children's fantasy novels under the collective moniker The Tales of Alegria, using the name LR Manley. They are *The Catastrophe of the Emerald Queen* and its sequel *The Sunder of the Octagon*. Both have strong anti-bullying themes and Lance has given talks in schools around the UK to promote them.

Now travelling the world and currently residing in Australia, *Cutting Off* is Lance's 11th book to date.

December 2016

∞ CUTTING OFF ∞

∞ CUTTING OFF ∞

Printed in Great Britain
by Amazon